Inklemaker

LISTENING FOR

Linda Dobbs has lived within sight of the sea on the Gower Peninsula, South Wales, for over twenty-five years. Throughout the early nineteen-fifties her homes were in London and Lancashire. She has vivid memories of a privileged childhood, often in the care of loving grandparents.

Now retired, Linda's writing is inspired by the frenetic concurrent careers she left as an office administrator, adult education tutor, 'moonlighting' dressmaker, and mother of three. Family history, travel, the Arts, life's joys and challenges, and Gower's great outdoors feature in this bitter-sweet, debut anthology.

Linda was awarded The Open University's Diploma in Literature & Creative Writing in 2010, and was shortlisted for her fiction entry to The Bridport Prize 2011.

Doreen MacNulty trained at Swansea School of Art. After graduation, she studied painting and stage design at The Slade School of Fine Art in London. Later, Doreen's move to West Africa influenced much of her work.

She now lives and works on Gower, and is interested in painting natural forms using vibrant colours, in both watercolour and pastels. Doreen exhibits frequently with several art groups and galleries.

Linda Dobbs

LISTENING FOR LIMPETS
A Personal Anthology

Inklemaker

Published in 2012 by *Inklemaker*
Trem y Môr, Port Eynon, Swansea SA3 1NL
email: inklemaker@aol.com

ISBN: 978-0-9546271-5-7

Copyright © Linda Dobbs 2012
Line Drawings © E. D. MacNulty
Limpet Digital Images © by kind permission of Jessica Winder

The right of Linda Dobbs to be identified as the author of this
work has been asserted by her in accordance
with the Copyright, Designs & Patents Act 1988

All rights reserved
No part of this publication may be reproduced, stored in a retrieval
system, or transmitted, in any form or by any means, electronic,
mechanical, photocopying, recording or otherwise, without the prior
consent of both the copyright owners
and their publisher

Printed in Wales by
Dinefwr Press Ltd, Llandybie, Carmarthenshire, SA18 3YD

Contents

Looking East From Rhossili Beacon 9
Something Mother Told Me 10
Entreaty 2009 12
Counterpane Snow 13
Singing Along With Doris 15
All Too Soon 19
Christmas Baby Blues 20
Longhole Cavechild 23
A Seasonal Enchantment 26
This Is Our A.O.N.B. 29

The Culver Hole Cache –
I – Discovery 33
II – Dragging Dink In Wellies 34
III – The Planning Stage 36
IV – Culver Hole 37
V – The Portrait 38
VI – Point Warning 39
VII – About Itself 40
VIII – Squatting 46
IX – The Lament Of The Salthouse Scullerymaid 49
X – Listening For Limpets 51

Winter Journey 53
How To Grow A Ski Champion 54
Chance Encounter In France 59
Hunting The Worm from Pennard Castle 61
Inside Out 63
Synchrony Inspired By A New Tank 65

The Garden Angel 66
The Leaving 68
Journey 71
The Cockfosters Terrorists 72
To The Better End 73
Seascape Characters – Oxwich Beach 75
Workout Worship 77
A Bump On The Head 79
Alphabet Of Summer 2003 Expansion 80
How To Be A Writer 83
Pretending 84
Clifftop Trees 86
Dropping One Dimension 88
One Pink Dianthus 89
Stouthall Buttercups 94
The Solicitous Limpet 95
Sixty 97
The Test Of Time 98
On Getting On, Not Getting Off 100
Toad In The Hole 102
Looking Back – September 2003 103
All Present And Correct 105
Passage 111
Bryn Mist 112
Warm November 2011 114
Sunset, Sleepless 117
Victim 118
Making Room 119
Elegy 125
Capture 126

*Yet, by your gracious patience,
I will a round unvarnish'd tale deliver.*

(Othello, The Moor of Venice, Act 1, Scene iii, by William Shakespeare)

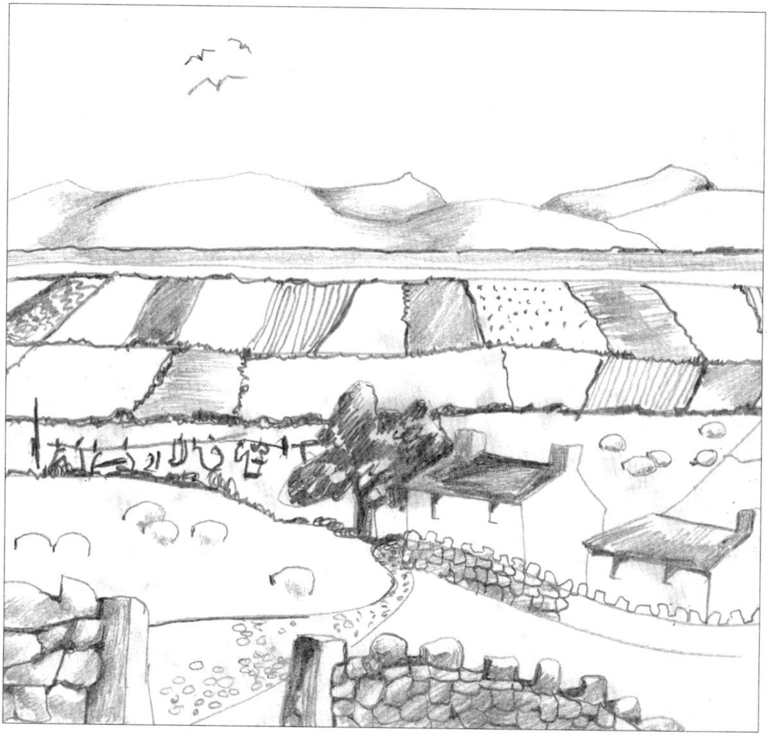

LOOKING EAST FROM RHOSSILI BEACON

I ramble to the Down's trig point, alone.
Then yearn to share the scene that lies beneath
the buzzard skimming creviced walls, soon flown
toward our cobalt canopy. The brief
fluting of pipits, the bleating of sheep,
and a skylark's warbling, sweet partita
prompt rhythms for laundered linens to leap
in gorse-perfumed breeze. Stout hedgerows – sweeter
for sloe blossom, bluebells, precocious may –
divide hectares into pristine patches;
this vast Gower counterpane drops away
to the sea's margin. Noon's spring tide crashes.
The Brecon Beacons beckon; hazy, blue.
I long for you to share this timeless view.

SOMETHING MOTHER TOLD ME...

It's easy for them to sneak in. Aunt Ethel leaves the door ajar most of the day, just in case. The spider in the corner nearest the house seems happy to be there; straddling the plate-sized web until it dashes down into the darkest recesses of our nightly 'thing to do' to terrorise the woodlice. Perhaps the woodlice feel the way we do; surprise spider attack from above. Scuttle away if you're lucky. Into the dark. Away from the sixteen feet which annihilate on contact.

Whether or not it pours all day, the air change is vital, especially when the Aunts come to us for shelter, their Highbury house flattened early on. So, we're eight now, here in South Harrow, or 'four and four halves, please'. That's the way I get through the night – we're on a cosy, open-topped bus tour. The conductor's given each of us a blanket and pillow. He brews tea on a camping stove to maintain routine when it's noisy outside. I concentrate on the weak blue flame, dismissing thoughts of the red-hot fire that raged, post-raid, through the Aunts' semi. They don't speak details while us 'halves' are around, which is all night, pressed up against the rippled metal walls, stacked two and two on the rough-hewn bunks, which shoot us with splinters if we're not careful. On our shelves we lay, teaspoons in a presentation case, not daring to roll over and no room to hoist heads, hoping night cramps won't affect us like they do Auntie Ethel, whose circulation suffers after five hours in her deckchair; no beds for the grown-ups.

We're dry and warm as moles beneath the low curved roof camouflaged with rear-lawn turfs. The bunch of us doesn't smell until morning. Night gases escape into the vegetable garden, lost amongst the brassicas. Cooled hot-water bottles are drained onto potato plants. I don't know where the covered bucket contents go, but throughout the summers from '41 to the end, the hollyhocks are magnificent.

We wear what we don at dusk, accustomed to the gloaming now: winceyette jamas covered by a woollen gown, socks, shoes; no possessions permitted in here. Six-year-old Janet doesn't understand that her teddy bear can sort itself out if it has to.

This is the new routine. Every night. Into the ground. Duck your nut. Don't leave your fingers behind for the heavy metal door to mash them. This is the place that Percy and the neighbours built. The only doubt they have is that we're five feet from the side of the house. The consequences of a direct hit to our leafy lane are never discussed. Night after night that same routine, hearing the Warden shout at Mr Pargeter next door for 'showing light'. Mr Pargeter's deaf. The Warden has a hard time getting through to him.

Our team becomes quickly used to the eight steps down from the terrace on the darkest of nights. We order ourselves smartly – a platoon under our RSM Mum, who shoves us up into the bunks.

We doze fitfully, eager for the 'all clear' around four or five in the dawning. When the raids are shorter, we can return to our beds in the half-light between dawn chorus and the milkman. On those days school starts later.

Before the evacuation lottery when, if you look good, you are swept away by inexperienced foster parents, the shelter is our family dormitory every night. No-one expects the daytime raids, when the brass-bold Luftwaffe strafes communities for sport. I will hear Ethel's brave voice until I die. She shouts to the land girls, screaming, terrified, gathering their apple harvest, in the orchard at our lane end.

'Get in the ditch. Get down in the ditch!' as a low-flying gunner lets rip from less than two hundred feet above our heads. There is little time to hide or hope on days like these.

Perhaps that's why the wood lice take their chances in our shelter, little knowing that the enemy will strike when they're least expecting it.

ENTREATY 2009
(Remembering Dan Joad)

Lifted last May, from the dark
Confines of his desiccated album,
After four-score years and twelve,
Jewel-bright scarlet, cobalt, sap,
Silk stitches shimmer.

Pansies tendril around
Nineteen-seventeen's
Allied Forces' rallying standards.

His plea – *Forget me not* – lingers
Within couched threads on tired Belgian lace
He kissed; embroidered on our hearts.

We read him, never forgetting his sacrifice.

COUNTERPANE SNOW

They recalled long, harsh winters
like none would ever see,
when movement was tough,
the darker nights cold,
and snow lay for weeks
heaped up by fences;
thick, and silencing
all but bird song.

They spoke about beds before
duvets and comforters,
when bolsters propped heads,
and potties saved trips
over wet ash pad
to a cold, wooden
plank over long drop;
cess pit below.

They mentioned Friday's tin bath
shared by each one in turn,
range-water steaming
from kettles on coals
baking spuds in skins,
lamb hotpot, dumplings,
what sixpence could buy,
trouble at Mill.

They listed thick wool blankets,
liberty bodices,
Great-Granddad's long johns,
sad and Eccles cakes,
Methodist chapel,
nights in bomb shelters,
the day alarmer,
clogs on cobbles.

They hankered after 'old days'
which they said 'were the best'
and won't come again.
They sang songs and hymns
in smoky parlours.
They slept beneath patched,
home-sewn counterpanes
when snow lay deep.

They moaned. Small voices as one
complained of the stifling
atmosphere, routine:
regretted their days
should cease within walls
not their own, not 'home';
the final refuge
they won't recall.

SINGING ALONG WITH DORIS
(For Mum)

'Sibble-O-two? Hello . . . .' Their grandchild's immature yelling confirms the connection to Western 7002, the telephone number of Dick and Olive's Kensington Mews flat. 'Housewives' Choice' is on Light and Doris Day is . . . *introdoocin Henry Miller* . . .

'Sibble-O-two? Hello . . .' Lindy adores her reflection in the oval sideboard mirror. Twin hair slides restrain her curly, shoulder-length hair, which her Nan throttled last night with torn strips of cotton from a redundant ironing cloth. Olive doesn't possess an ironing board. She prefers a folded blanket under a flannelette sheet, on the dining table. The mirror reflects the ordered chaos there. At one end, silk body-parts, still pinned to Vogue pattern pieces, await Olive's treadle or the steady stab-stitch of the basting needle. Her silver thimble flashes in filtered light through lacy nets. The apple box puppet theatre has been painted and Olive's made red velvet curtain swags, hammered on this morning by Granddad. Lindy has just three puppets for this weekend's show: Prince Charming (resembling King Charles I, eyebrow-pencilled black moustache, quill in bonnet); Queen Bess (plaited orange crewel wig, crown of pearls); and The Nurse (whose uniform is part of the same old ironing cloth, minus the brown singed bits, with crucifix of crimson bias binding). Lindy hasn't decided on a plot, but she'll find inspiration from somewhere and is determined Queen Bess will sing *My Secret Love,* because Lindy knows every word from Doris Day's latest release; has been rehearsing downstairs, at full pitch. She's a smidgen disappointed that the puppet faces are smooth, but that's too bad. At least there were enough Swan Vesta matchbox sleeves to make the puppet heads, and Olive's painted appropriate theatrical expressions on the trio.

A 'Blossom Time' five-hundred-piece jigsaw lies half-finished at the other end of the table. Tulips thrive, incongruously, in the garden of a traditional, high-alpine chalet, and mother waves to two blonde children in the garden. Lindy is barely five years old. She can assemble the puzzle – always tulips first – in the time it takes her Nan to prepare an evening dress for a first fitting for Mrs 'Robin Hood', or Mrs Donald Houston, provided Olive's not taking tea with Miss Bette Davis, who's on location in London and renting No. 24 Adam & Eve Mews.

The candlestick apparatus is necessary for Dick and Olive to run their two businesses from home and has been their one luxury here since 1936. The child has little idea of the use for the bell-end, which she holds and taps on the slide above her right ear. Olive is tickled by Lindy's confidence; takes the earpiece from her, unconcerned whether the caller's making a professional enquiry, or if it's Auntie Gertie taking Friday night's regular order for jellied eels.

Tomorrow, they're off to Olympia, to see Coco the Clown at Bertram Mills' Circus. Earl's Court's not a huge distance from the flat, but Dick will chauffeur them in the Austin Six and they'll sing *By the light of the silvery moon* as they trundle over the Mews cobbles. The Austin's more luxurious than the taxi cab (and Lindy likes to pretend powdering her nose with the pom-pom bobbles of its sun blinds). As Granddad drives the cab every day, he deserves a change every so often.

Olive took Lindy to Regent's Park Zoo last week; she doesn't bother with nearby Holland Park as there's little to interest the child.

Most afternoons, Olive abandons the sewing, dons her roll-ons, and the pair walk up the Mews to the High Street, and turn towards Kensington Gardens. A narrow alley backs onto all the shops and offices west of Pontings. Olive strides along the High Street, past the 'Adam & Eve' and Dolcis, whilst Lindy scampers along the parallel alleyway, past dustbins, stacked empty bottle crates, and rear doors of the units, then jumps out to surprise Olive in the tiled cool of the atrium, Kensington High Street Station, Circle Line. Then they cross the High Street at the traffic

Entreaty – forget me not – WWI postcard

Winter journey – the Mont Blanc from Chamonix

lights, and pass the Town Hall. Steamy suet smells swirl through basement skylight vents in the bottle-glass pavement, on which Lindy tap dances. St. Mary Abbott's nursery school is tranquil in the afternoon sun. They stroll up Church Street with its chic antique shops, upholstery and tailoring studios, window boxes blooming rainbows. Olive seems to know everyone and introduces Lindy to a woman – sunning herself on the stoop – whose shop window's embellished by an enormous sterling silver tea set, which Olive covets.

'How much is the tea set, Nan? Why don't you ask Granddad to buy it for you?' The child's nose butts the shop window. Her breath fogs the plate glass. Her pudgy finger traces a Sheriff's badge in the condensation. Lindy never asks Granddad to buy *her* things. Treasures just present themselves whenever she stays at No. 18 and are stacked on the sideboard: a Diablo set; a rubber dolly which tiddles through its neck, arm and leg joints (after Lindy used Olive's pinking shears to excise the tube joining mouth to 'nappy end'); and three old books, which once belonged to Penelope Rubenstein whose name is pencilled inside the front covers. Lindy knows every word of 'The Little House' and 'Orlando the Marmalade Cat'. 'The Favourite Wonder Book' includes an epic poem – 'The Wreck of the Steamship Puffin' – describing a storm on The Round Pond in Kensington Gardens, where Lindy sometimes sails a model boat in fine weather.

Olive's oblivious, imagining the silver arrayed on her dining room mantelpiece. No. 18 is full of treasures. The best, and of endless fascination to Lindy, is Nan's gold belcher bracelet, dripping with more than fifty gold charms. The child has asked Olive if the bracelet can be hers when Olive dies soon (because Nan seems old, though she's in her early forties; Dick's third wife, and stepmother to Lindy's mum). The bracelet's protected overnight in a velvet-lined treasure box built of bevelled crystal. Lindy likes to see her peachy reflection in that mirror surface, too. She's not allowed to touch the box because Uncle George (who made it for Nan) would be cross if it broke.

Olive uses an oval, beaten copper tray to stop up the snug's chimney during summer months. Lindy's distorted midget reflection bounces back at her from the beaten copper. Dick cleans it, and the front door furniture, with Brasso every Tuesday. Lindy has her own duster to help buff the treasures. She worries that Granddad polishes the door handle too much; he's steadily removing the black gloss surrounding the brass bits. No matter how hard Lindy rubs, a genie never appears.

Today, they're visiting Kensington Palace Museum. Here, Olive confuses Lindy about kings and queens; explains that old Queen Mary was the new Queen's Nan. Lindy is interested in queens, particularly since seeing the old Queen's funeral, and the coronation of young Elizabeth, who's only a couple of years older than Lindy's mummy. The child wishes her mummy could be Queen, and that they could both ride in the gold coach she saw from her damp perch on Granddad's shoulders, last drizzly June.

She wanders with Olive through the Palace's State Apartments wondering how often visitors sleep in the huge four-poster beds, which look so uncomfortable. In the basement, they see stuffed animals, the Palace porcelain collection, and a dreary exhibition of George Robey memorabilia. And, lastly, Lindy heads for the glass case containing her favourite exhibit: Anna Pavlova's tutu, headdress, and scuffed ballet shoes she wore as 'The Dying Swan'. Olive explains that Pavlova gave the costume to the Museum when she came to live in London after the First World War, but Lindy can't understand why Pavlova doesn't still dance in all those feathers.

Lindy hopes that, one day, she'll be a famous ballet dancer. Meanwhile, she goes on rehearsing her version of *The Deadwood Stage* from *Calamity Jane*. Only Olive can hear her singing and dancing in No. 18's empty basement garage, so it doesn't matter if a word or two is wrong. At least, the tune's off pat and Lindy can join in with Doris Day every time Doris sings inside Granddad's wireless.

(Two 101-word pieces inspired by
'Anthropology – 101 True Love Stories' by Dan Rhodes)

ALL TOO SOON

Poppy presented Remembrance Sunday, eleventh November. Later, during Songs of Praise, she burbled verses to *Melita*; harmonised the choruses.

On Monday, Poppy vaulted her cot railings, dressed, then took Bertie basset for his constitutional.

Came Tuesday evening, we couldn't sustain Poppy's pace. She'd gone to school at eight o'clock, stayed late for Youth Club. Not just her time-keeping concerned us.

Wednesday, Poppy mobile-phoned from a squat: it was 'interesting to be independent, hungry'. Might we spare some dosh?

Poppy landed a job, Thursday, then confessed she'd take maternity leave that weekend.

Friday, Poppy's baby boy arrived.

Her challenge started that Saturday.

CHRISTMAS BABY BLUES

Fragile child, unknowing,
I've spent just five days
  guarding you growing
  into baggy skin,
  blotched, battered face;
  stunned by the hell
  you raise when
  you need me.

We're firm friends now.
I gossip at you, content
  there's no response;
  just puckered lips
  practising blown kisses,
  startled brows,
  or steady breathing
  as you slumber.

We're homeward-bound today.
The Army's carolling,
  brass bright in Christmas sun,
  as Dad shares the fun
  of clothing you in
  outsize bonnet, bootees.
  He wraps you warm
  against the winter breeze.

You're cradled tight.
I shed plump tears
 upon your shawl:
 a first-time mum
 fearful for us all.

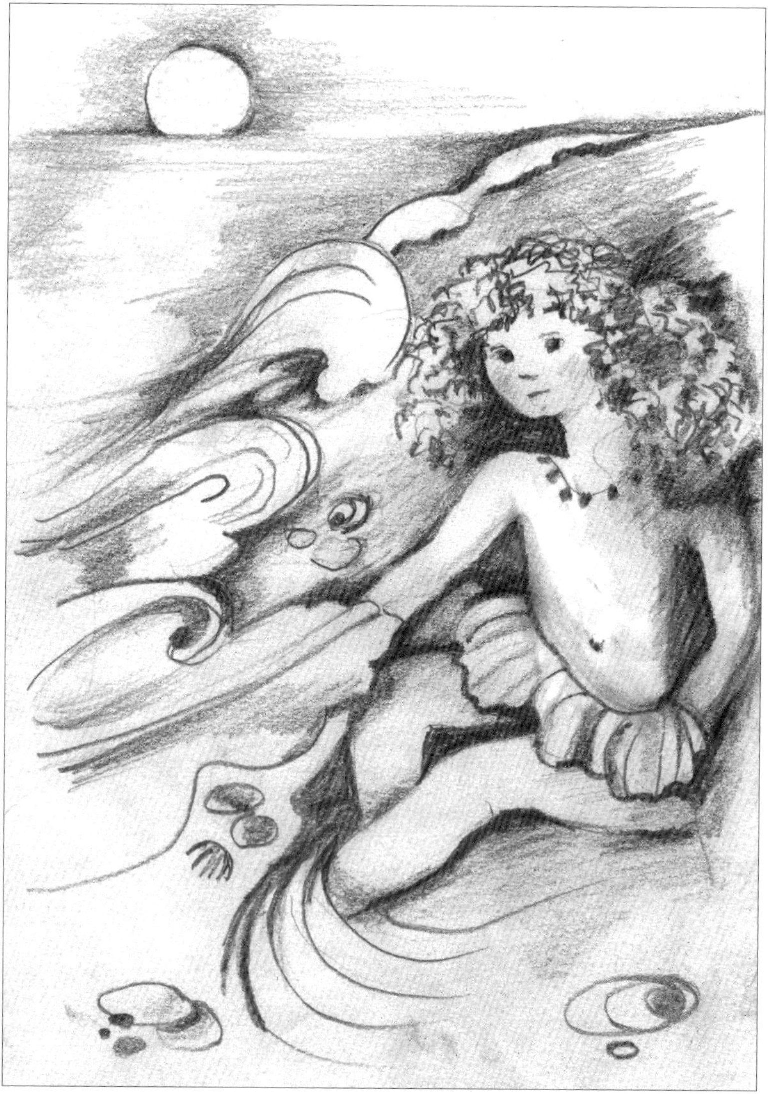

LONGHOLE CAVECHILD

Known to have been occupied by man since the Stone Age, Longhole Cave lies west of Port Eynon, Gower, high above the sea in an accessible cliff.

Startled from deep sleep by a searching moon
and surging stones on an insistent tide
battering our bay – hurling weed as waves
engorge, rear up to collapse, spent, on sand –
we tremble at the sea's majesty; sigh,
warm yet wondering, sheltered in this cave.

The gods forbid these limestone cliffs should cave
in to obliterate the stars and moon;
that our ears cease to hear stooped, gnarled trees sigh
in breezes driven by a restless tide.
We harvest stout driftwood, scoured in harsh sand;
bleached white, beached daily by incessant waves.

Our child has keener senses now. She waves
from her vantage point west of our weird cave:
cute offspring shaping sea serpents from sand;
harvesting laver from dawn 'til the moon
shines; fishing shell food marooned by the tide
in fathomless pools. She hears limpets sigh.

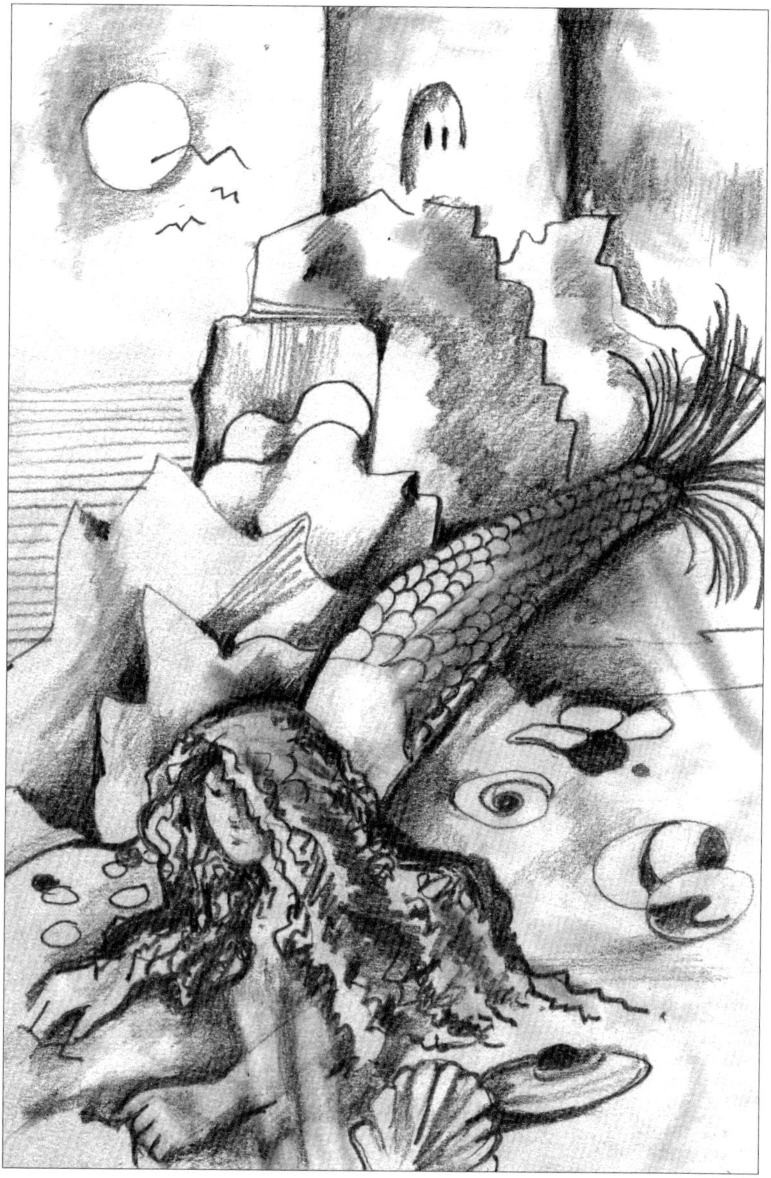

She drew her first breath. She exhaled a sigh.
We cleansed her perfection in timid waves
licking our beach on that springtime neap tide.
Couched on moss, bracken, she slept in our cave
high on the cliff's face. She sang to the moon.
She moulded Her full features from wet sand.

We threaded tellins littered on that sand
adorned our babe, eliciting her sigh,
unaware we had lost her to a Moon
omnipotent as rough, relentless waves
pounding their rhythms on our shore. The cave
remained our refuge; hers, the rising tide.

She plunges from a rock washed by high tide;
her skin sheds minute particles of sand
that sparkle in bright summer sun. This cave
is no longer her home, haven. We sigh.
We ponder, as she dives beneath the waves,
do we mean as much to her as her Moon?

Sunbeams drown the moon. Cliff-top grasses sigh.
Midnight's wild waves – calmer now – lap damp sand.
Close by our cave, her scaled fin scythes the tide.

A SEASONAL ENCHANTMENT

'Twas the week before Christmas. The tree had been dressed.
Baubles glistened in branches, but Mum was depressed,
for the list she'd been keeping, of jobs she'd to do,
had dropped from her pinny, on a trip to the loo.
Down the lav, round the bend, went the list with a rush!
She kicked herself wondering, *Oh! why did I flush?*
For the list, with details of cute stocking fillers,
fruit, veg, and sherry, and Dad's paperback thrillers,
was vital: her plan noting matters essential,
and without it Christmas had little potential.
It would take her all year to start over again.
Christmas planning was just like a battle campaign,
with names due for greeting cards, parcels and parties,
and notes on sponge cakes, needing icing and Smarties,
times for preparation, stuffing, cooking and such.
She'd even allowed time for spring-cleaning the hutch,
while the rabbit came in for its Christmas cuddle.
Would she ever get straight from this frightful muddle?

She read the list yesterday, whilst drinking coffee,
taking a break from manufacturing toffee,
but could only recall unusual shopping.
This week would be rushed. There'd be no time for stopping.
Mum slumped in her chair, sighed a sigh, felt defeated.
Without her list, how could her plans be completed?
Then she shouted out loud, in a huge fit of pique,
'What a dope I am? How will I cope all this week?
I need help. Is there anyone out there for hire?'

And she jumped as she heard 'Just what do you desire?'
The words came from out of thin air, sweet as honey,
from the Christmas, life-saving, Fairy-Godmummy.
She sparkled to life from a twinkling tree bauble
and, with a comforting voice, started to warble,

'You're not stupid, my child. Just a tired, worn-out wife,
who has never sought personal space in this life
far away from the duties which Christmas entails;
when you're always expected to have well-groomed nails
and serve turkey and trimmings and mountains of grub,
when the kids and their Dad stagger back from the pub.
I will magic a spell. Close your eyes. Hold your breath,'
(at which words, Mum reflected, she felt scared to death!)
The plump Fairy waved her wand, breathed 'Izzy-wizzy,
and come, festive spirits, to work – let's get busy.'

In a waft of warm air spiced with orange and cloves,
and a delicate tinkling of tiny gold hooves,
rode an army of pixies, on reindeer, held fast
by the kindly ghost we know as Old Christmas Past,
who reminded tired Mum of long-gone childhood joys
and the wonder of opening stocking-wrapped toys,
gold chocolate coins, almonds, walnuts, and Spangles,
petticoats, hair slides, bubblebath, and gold bangles.
The reindeer cavalcade tapped out melodies sweet
as they pranced around the room on musical feet,
and in what seemed a trice Mum's worries disappeared
as Santa emerged with a gleaming snowy beard.

Santa greeted Fairy-Godmum, squeezing her tight.
'We can finish the tasks from the lost list tonight.'
And he charged the pixies to fulfil Mum's wishes;
by the end of that spell, fridge crammed with dishes,
parcels bought, wrapped and labelled, stashed into a sack,
and the rabbit well fed, in the clean hutch out back.
They laundered all the washing, and polished floor tiles,
and throughout this hard work all the pixies wore smiles.

As the grandfather clock chimed a half-hour past ten,
Mother started and drowned in her sorrows again.
But her eyes grew like saucers as she looked around,
in a trance, not believing the neatness she found.

Then she remembered Fairy Godmum's last warning:
'Don't speak of the magic before ten next morning.
If you tell tales to folks, they'll think you quite crazy,
not to mention puffed up, and probably lazy.
Pixies are diligent when occasions demand,
but they'll make your life hell on my given command.
So keep your lips sealed, forget our visit this night.'
Then, the Fairy turned into a bauble so bright.

Now Mum smiles when she recalls why magic occurred.
What's her secret of Christmas success?
Mum's the word.

THIS IS OUR A.O.N.B.

This is our A.O.N.B.

This is the coast
That circles our A.O.N.B.

These are the bays
Adorning the coast
That circles the A.O.N.B.

These are the folks
Who like the bays
That adorn the coast,
That circles our A.O.N.B.

These are the cars
That bring the folks,
Who like the bays
Bejewelling the coast,
That circles the A.O.N.B.

These are the queues, on a summer's morn,
Formed by the cars

Carrying folks
Who like the bays
That adorn the coast,
That circles our A.O.N.B.

This is a driver full of scorn,
Fuming in queues and sounding his horn
At all the cars,
That bring the folks
Who like the bays,
That adorn the coast
That circles the A.O.N.B.

This is the youngster, eating popcorn –
Child of the driver stifling a yawn,
Fuming in queues and sounding his horn
At all the cars
Bringing the folks
Who like the bays,
That adorn the coast,
That circles their A.O.N.B.

This is the packet, soggy and torn,
Tossed by the youngster, who's hogged the popcorn,
Ignored by his Pa stifling a yawn,
Fuming in queues and sounding his horn
At all the cars that bring the folks

Who like the bays
That adorn the coast
That circles this A.O.N.B.

This devastation we all should mourn.
Dispose of trash redundant and worn
That's lobbed by our youngsters who've hogged popcorn
While irate Pa smothers a yawn.
He's fuming in queues and sounding his horn
At all the cars
That bring the folks
Who like the bays,
That adorn the coast
That circles his A.O.N.B.

Gower sun breaks through a mist-filled dawn,
Spotlighting mess (we've *begun* to mourn)
Made by leaving trash redundant and worn,
Discarded by youngsters fed on pop corn
By Dad. He does little but yawn,
Livid in tailbacks, sounding his horn
At all the cars
That bring the folks,
Who like the bays
Adorning the coast,
That circles this A.O.N.B.

THE CULVER HOLE CACHE

One of two on Gower named 'Culver Hole', the deep cleft in Port Eynon Point's undercliff is heavily fortified by a masonry wall with two doors and a circular window, and is believed to have served one of two, or perhaps both, purposes: a smuggler stronghold to store contraband brought, at high water, into the cliff's difficult approach, or a pigeonry where eggs and birds might be captured to supplement a fisherman's diet in the early to mid-eighteenth century.

Culver Hole is a favourite tourist location and is pictured in many guidebooks on Britain's coastline. At low water in Overton Mere, with a steep scramble access on each side of the cliff approach, the remains of a staircase inside the masonry can be accessed through an upper doorway above the fluctuating beach level, which has gradually buried the original sea entrance over the past twenty-five years. The Hole is the roost for jackdaws, pigeons and smaller birds, and their calls echo eerily around the walls in the early evening . . .

The one-eyed pirates' lair, Culver Hole, Overton Mere

Salt House ruins, Port Eynon Bay

I – DISCOVERY

I still remember finding her that day,
decades ago, when limbs and heart were strong.
The site of her there – walls dull pewter-grey –
perfect. There's nowhere else she could belong.
Enigma was the word which came to mind.
She is no folly; built so strong to last.
There were no contracts, documents men signed
of Title. She's a relic of their past;
ancestral roost to creatures on the wing,
withstanding tides and storms that scour her stones.
And if she found a voice, what would she sing?
Of sea frets, smugglers, skeletons' bleached bones?
Immutable through centuries long gone,
I wonder, has she strength to carry on?

-o-

II – DRAGGING DINK IN WELLIES
(In memory of Mother-in-law)

We started out one morning,
the five of us and Dink.
We told Nan that she ought to wear thick socks.
The kids all wore their trainers
and the parents sported boots
to save our feet from suffering on rocks.

We packed a flask, and Penguins
to eat along the way.
The kids, delighted, set off with broad smiles.
But Dink hung back, reluctant.
She said she'd feel a fool
in wellies, in the sunshine, walking miles.

The kids said, 'Nan, don't worry.
You'll not look off your head.
Don't forget the factor ten for your face.'
The great adventure started
by skirting round the Point
and leaving with the tide to find the place.

We'd read so much about it;
had lived close by for years.
The map showed just exactly where to look.
It took us hours to struggle
over pools, rocks and stones.
Then we reached the site: some impressive nook!

Dink flopped down on a boulder,
and let her hairdo breathe.
She sighed and said we'd have to 'put her down'.
She couldn't face the battle,
to climb back up the cliff,
and argued she was 'quite prepared to drown'.

Her problem was the wellies.
They'd blistered both her heels.
She couldn't bear the thought of painful nights.
She paddled in a puddle.
(The tide was too far out.)
Inside the boots, our Nan had worn old tights!

The moral to this story
is simple. Don't take Nans
on expeditions where they cannot cope.
But if you don't discover,
until it's far too late,
they're knackered, then be sure to take a rope.

-o-

III – THE PLANNING STAGE

'We're gonna lug
some stones to wall
a hideout,' says Lucas.

'It'll be a
modest project,
starting next month's neap tide
and ending when
I think it's high enough.

We'll stash all the
hot stuff, lolly
best kept outdoors, in case
the bastard's raid
us while we sleep.
There's a perfect fissure
under the Point
and, if we build it well,
in centuries
it could become
Port Eynon's enigma.'

'Not sure as we
knows what you means,
Lucas,' sighs Tom Beynon,
chewing a straw,
arms crossed, dismissively.

IV – CULVER HOLE

The smugglers' one-eyed lair peers through the cleft.
She longs to hear the slap of waves on hulls.
Her heart is broken, centuries bereft;
within, the stench of flotsam. Screaming gulls
confuse her brow left yawning at the sky.
With boulders racked by storm, her mouth stopped tight
permits no ingress, has no means to sigh
to soothe the pigeons roosting through dark night.
Her nostril accepts visitors, who climb
two fathoms at low tide to mourn her doom.
The lair will swallow those with little time
who fall within her flesh, lost in the gloom.
The one-eyed lair holds fast against the foam.
The *raison d'etre* is known to her alone.

-o-

V – THE PORTRAIT

'Paint *me*', she begs,
so close that I
can discern her
foetid gasp from
ozone on the breeze.

Pent-up for years,
her yearning plea
startles the birds,
fluttering to
lift above the cliff.

I scan the stones.
The window, door
are bare of all
but dark shadows.
The birds have found trees.

The walled inlet
is deserted;
has been so since
high tide allowed
sea access by skiff.

Intrigued, hake poised,
loaded cobalt
dropping in sky

where ocean should
be wet-washed, I freeze.
I still my breath,
then loosely paint
a rising tide
lapping the wall
where Culver's ghosts live.

-o-

VI – POINT WARNING

She hears the warning buoy begin to sound.
A southerly – persistent – stirs sea thrift
posies in limestone clefts, on squill-specked ground.

The buoy bleats. No specific tonal shift;
just the Mere's hint, its wavelets raising foam.
Strong tidal swell encourages the notes
to lighten. And the bell begins to moan;
its plaintive wail a warning that their boat
must steer away from wrecking rocks beneath
that scour then splinter. Out there in the gloom
the sailors steer their craft, in God their faith.
The Salt House mermaid croons her eerie tune.

She hears the ship's bell clanging upon deck.
She waits for death; rich plunder from the wreck.

VII – ABOUT ITSELF

Unlike other architectural relics
with some pedigree,
the local authority aren't keen
to preserve what's left
of me.

Inside, I'm decaying at a faster rate
than outside, where it's
purgatory in a force seven
or more.

It's my base that's suffering most.
The crash of stones
and boulders – no matter
how smoothly rounded – at
high tide is like a
civil war bombardment:
heavy shot from
a cannon.

The voracious storm of 1698
devoured the underbelly of
Port Eynon Point
and left the limestone
overhang impassable
from above.

I can't be seen from the land.
The concave cutting,
undercliff, makes it
impossible to look into
my depths.

When they started the infill wall
I was astounded. They used
the westerly approach, and
stones were finished on site.
The mason did a good job.
The wall's been here for about
three centuries. I've
lost count.

I see all-comers. From the water,
few. They pass, cocooned in
bright colours, legless,
whirring paddles.
We stare at each other –
me, wondering why they're
so free of ballast and
high on the waves;
they, pondering on the
folly, or ingenuity, which
made me.

I hear them coming.
I see them coming; nervous

at first, then with a
determined reserve.
They start their descent from the
western approach, where the
worn footpath trickles away,
indistinct and scattered
across lichen-covered
terraces; hell
in winter.

The final slide into my
narrow cove has been polished
down the decades
by the passage of padded flesh.
In the beginning, there was
a firm scaffolding to support
the drop of stones and
Lucas's men.

They laboured through
long evenings in June,
no lights needed.
Besides, they weren't keen
to attract interest or
attention to the project
in hand.

Now, the inquisitive contort
themselves to reach polished footholds and,
mostly, land safely on knee-deep flotsam

marooned by retreating tides.
Every few years, my lower
portal is revealed and
summer tourists stumble
across pebbles
and bladderwrack to
see inside.

They are disillusioned.
My floors were taken for firewood
when the game was finally up,
and the authorities knew best
how to discourage
wreckers and their
Salt House associates,
who'd been using
the stash.

My internal stairway
should have been demolished.
It's never clear of guano; a
treacherous path for those
seeking adventure.

Someone ties a new hemp line
to my tidal doorway every year,
guaranteeing that those with
good muscles and faith in
their balancing ability
can invade.

They like to pose at the circular window;
my eye on the
North Devon coast,
across the channel leading
to Bristol.

Birds are my most regular visitors.
I've spotted jackdaw
pigeons, kittiwakes,
blackbirds, and I'm waiting
for choughs to investigate.

They seem fairly happy
at Pennard, but may come
out west.

I'm pissed off with folks
pissing in me. Rubbish
deposited is scant. It's
the jetsam which
invariably finds its
storm-driven,
winter-way in.

A commune who tried me
gave up after two weeks.
Weather was their enemy
and damp on the stairs
caused dissent.
They've since built a

pavilion at Slade,
for summer months,
preferring the sandy beach
to torture
crossing the rock
platform running south.
In the winter, it's been whispered,
they've taken possession of
a barge somewhere.

Reams have been written about me
in guide books, pamphlets.
But no-one really knows
what I'm
all about.

I'd like to be maintained,
but not in the way they used to
when I was full of stuff
they were hiding from the
Excise men. Then again, some organised
person could increase the
pigeon population and
do a roaring trade in
pigeon pies.

That would make a pleasant
change from fish and chips
by the seafront
or pudding and peas from The Ship.

VIII – SQUATTING

'You'll need a head for heights.'
Some know-all who'd been there
had accepted a dare;
been inside without lights.

'The tide needs to be down,
or risk an anchored boat
to keep the gear afloat.
You wouldn't want to drown.'

Agreed. We'd try at ten
to make the folly ours.
We tramped there in showers;
brought damp into the den.

A rope hung from the door.
We tested it for strength
but moaned about its length.
It wouldn't reach the floor.

'We'll have to build some stairs
and hoist them up inside,'
our know-all leader cried.
'The place needs some repairs.'

At first we felt at home:
a famous squat address.
But illness brought distress;
the know-all first to moan.
'The birds are bloody loud.
I haven't slept for days.
I'm thinking, too, of ways
we might reduce this crowd.'

We tensed and looked around:
a happy commune – free.
All kids who loved the sea,
feet firm on solid ground.

We voted know-all out.
She slid down from the door
and waded to the shore.
No more her heavy clout.

We sat around next day,
expressions dour, morose.
The know-all was verbose.
We'd nothing left to say.

We stayed there just two weeks.
Our food stocks ran right down.
We caught the bus to town
and dined on Jaffa cakes.

There's someone new in charge.
We need a figure-head
who won't just laze in bed.
Now we squat on a barge.

-o-

IX – THE LAMENT OF THE SALTHOUSE SCULLERYMAID

He promised me the moon and stars that night.
I'd heard it all before, but played along;
assured the ship was loaded with rich freight.
He wanted me to sing a mermaid's song,
as lanterns lured from deep within the gloom.
There'd be reward enough to change my life.
I wanted him; his seed within my womb
was planted, though I'd not become his wife.
We trod the limestone crag without embrace
or kiss, or whispered sigh. The path was clear.
He urged me on, to slide into that space
where days before we'd frolicked by the Mere.
He drowned that night, cupidity the cause.
My son aborted. I'm still swabbing floors.

-o-

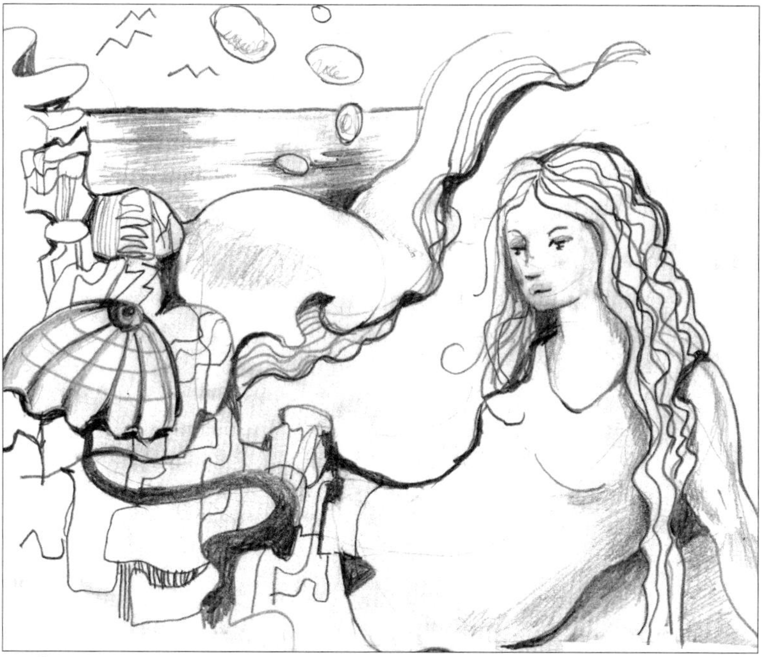

X – LISTENING FOR LIMPETS
(For Jessica)

Hunkered in a Skysea rocky cleft –
sun scorching, mid-September,
what remains of once-golden sands
glistening after tide's retreat –
bellows pushed and pulled here,
in my two-row D/G squeezebox,
relieve villagers
of a cacophony,
as digits endeavour to master
Captain Pugwash's *Trumpet* Hornpipe.

Hidden from sight – silent, light breezes
dancing down Port Eynon's Point
to riffle hairs on suntanned arms –
my heart's content is to be here
among mollusc remains:
sifting shingle for lost treasure;
snapping seashore hues
to ward off winter's gloom;
tracing vapour trails displayed on blue;
teasing tiddlers, shrimps, in tidal pools.

Hearing a faint gasp, I rise to scan
pitted scarps and dips close by,
but see no sign of sentient souls
on beach, cliffs or Salt House ruins.
But surely something moaned!
Stilled breath, heart beating audibly,

straining to listen,
I hear a subdued sigh
seep from a gastropod adhering
to its home scar yearning for tide-turn.

WINTER JOURNEY
(For Clare Pearson)

Our slip-stitched ribbon road glows in moonshine
from indigo twilight twinkling with dust
like rare diamonds. Plantations of pine
slide silently by; trunks rooted in crust
on deep drifts seared by the sun then frozen.
This landscape horizon's jagged summits –
a destination thoughtfully chosen
for sublime majesty and snow that plummets
from mountain pass to pastures lying fallow –
beckon and beguile, whether the season's
filled with wild flowers or leaves burnished gold.
To list the endless detail, or reasons,
would take many words. Yet, though we grow old,
we'll journey each year to the deep alpine cold.

HOW TO GROW A SKI CHAMPION

Just outside the Chamonix Valley lie some enchanting, and less demanding, family ski resorts which provide a gentle, rolling contrast to the Valley's jagged peaks and extreme, off-piste playgrounds. The Mont Blanc Range's foothills bask in high-season winter sunshine and hold well their snow for those months of the year, enabling budding novices to perfect their techniques, or the very young members of the local community to commence their Alpine initiation.

Where British mothers will purchase a supply of stepped-size separates to cater for the first two years of their children's lives, the mothers of the *Haute-Savoie* go several steps fluffier and clothe their offspring in the most exquisite, down-filled ski gear, for all daily activities. Nappies seem never to need changing, button noses never drip, and the suit bibs stay immaculate all day – no dribble or reflux solids under dimpled chins.

The casual visitor here will find little evidence of the newborn baby. *Savoyard* offspring are believed to have a fourteen month gestation period, and are presented as staggering toddlers, who instinctively seem utterly content to sit in, scoop up and suck, slide over, and throw the white soft stuff that dominates their outdoor world from the end of October until the following spring.

Tiny French alpine downhill champions cut their teeth on minute, leather, designer mittens which are soggy and usually, therefore, frozen stiff, dangling on safety strings from inside the cosy cuffs of their all-in-ones. These 'puffball' outfits are quite delightful to behold – baggy, colourful, warm, never mass-produced – with matching detachable hoods, furry collars and incorporated scarves designed to muffle the shoulders, necks, chins and mouths of the little folk, rather more to keep them as warm as a welcoming glass of *vin chaud* than to stifle their whines of protest after a demanding day in the Snowpark with an understanding ski instructor.

Pulled or pushed by doting relatives of all ages, the little people travel about in sturdy, brightly-coloured plastic skidoos lined with blankets or fur. Their feet are shod in dumpy, insulating moon-boots to match the yellows, reds, mauves and whites of their plastic 'snowmobiles'. Their eyes are protected from the glare of the intense winter sun on high, and from the snow surrounding them, by outsized glacier glasses (some with mirror-reflector lenses) or scaled-down ski goggles. When little people gather together in groups of five or more, one is inevitably drawn to the veiled eyes of what appears to be a swarm of outsize blue-bottles.

All *Savoyard* toddler noses are button-sized, snubbed and bright pink. They protrude from just above the top level of the wrapped-around scarves. You rarely see a toddler mouth, but invariably will hear the sounds the little people make, in no uncertain fashion, at set times of the day. Early morning 'delight' gurgles are evident from between the hours of nine-thirty and lunchtime. Early *après midi* 'protest' noises follow between the hours of thirteen- to fifteen-hundred. From then onwards, the range can fluctuate considerably from quiet whimpering through insistent grizzling and on to loud bellowing, as the little alpine devotees give in to the fatigue brought on by constant activity in bracing mountain air.

Tiny tots are encouraged to slide along upon candyfloss pink miniskis, but their reflex response is to attempt to march in them, in spite of the constant tutor-commentary coming at them from a strong Daddy at their rear, suspending them by the armpits and posing simultaneously for the *Savoyard* Mummy to video his antics.

Beyond toddler stage, the 'Terrible Twos & Threes' and 'Fearless Fours & Fives' are moulded into crack shot ski teams, ever-destined to snake downhill in long threadlike lines, dutifully attempting to mimic their *ESF* ski tutor. The ubiquitous protecting dark lenses are, by this stage, usually outsize designer ski goggles and parents recognise their offspring by names emblazoned on the rear of their skisuits, or stamped upon the Formula One crash helmets which turn each of the heads into giant billiard balls. Some teams spend all school-day in the snowplough position descending at twenty miles an hour plus, and scaring stupid us older participants of the sport, with their ability to out-manoeuvre their peers when the teacher's attention is momentarily off-guard. The crack shots appear, seemingly out of nowhere or – at least – out of the bright setting sunset, in a gust of icy wind, and slide over larger skis in the lift queue to take their places for a final downhill *red* and then home for supper. There are some truly bright 'sparks' among these ski hopefuls, who might well rely on a gymnastics career if they fail at downhill prowess. They lark about with ski-hoist poles, or hang precariously from the retaining bars of chairlifts. They break all the ski-lift rules and glide out of the tracks and into the off-piste powder, straining the lift system to its limit and the tempers of the adults who wished they could do the same if they had enough 'bottle'.

Without the care, guidance and infinite patience of the ski school instructor, the staggering stragglers in the Nursery Snow-park could never aspire to success on the slopes. After mother and father have drummed into their child that skis are for sliding upon and not for waving about on the ends of stamping feet, it is time for their little protégé to join his or her peers in a little bunch of beginners, corralled on the lower nursery field. One cannot use the term 'slope', because it would be more than the instructor's life was worth to allow any of the tinies to slide off into infinity without proper control of the equipment in which they've been abandoned, so that their parents can tour the whole resort of Megeve for the day ahead. The toddlers are deposited in the Nursery enclosure, containing man-size models of penguins, polar bears, marmots and performing seals, along with various child-size two-dimensional Disney cartoon obstacles designed to test their knee-bending capabilities, as they stagger through the arches cut out of Goofy's or Mickey's or Donald's bodies. Presumably, the psychologists have given much consideration to the calming influence of a lovable Disney character, after the toddlers have been scared witless by the towering marmots and penguins dotted about the place.

The grizzling begins – and fast gathers hysterical momentum – as the toddlers are planted on the *piste* and told *'au revoir'* by their keepers. They cannot run after their loved ones with their feet heavily encased in Salomon clip-boots and secured tidily to the latest Salomon bindings and skis. Sausage-like arms wave in protest. The ski instructor begins his soothing assurances about the fun that will ensue, the little champions they will all become (or is that *champignons*?), and how 'today, we will all learn how to sidestep'.

There's lots of unsteady sliding around, with some of the youngsters wobbling over onto padded backsides and obstructing the progress of a peer following on behind. The instructor has his work cut out and obtains his inner glow from the effort to set upright those who've fallen by the wayside. After about one hour, all the tots are successfully marshalled – shoulder to shoulder in a row – on an orange mat which has been laid out upon the crisp white snow, with plastic, primary-coloured traffic cones at each end.

'Now,' enthuses the instructor, 'we can all side step, like this to the end of the mat' and he plants alternate ski poles, stepping instep to instep, sideways along his patch of *piste*. Rather like a string of cut out dollies in a pleated-paper row, the children are quick to imitate their teacher. Almost as one, the eleven pairs of tiny ski-boots and skis click and rattle sideways, step after step, as the toddlers progress crabwise from the red and green cones up to the yellow and blue.

Doting guardians beam their smiles from the Snowpark boundary fence and there are cries of 'Bravo, Juliette. Bravo, Nicholas' and muffled applause from mitten-clad hands striking together in the crisp, late afternoon. These congratulations are not so much for the offspring as for recognition of the infinite patience and tenderness of the ski instructor, who beams back and hurriedly replants two very young tumblers who, having crashed into each other, have no verbal means to express their annoyance and are now punching each other, ineffectively, about their glossy helmets.

In the crowd, a drowsy 'newborn' – one of the fourteen-month-olds mentioned earlier – pokes a chilly thumb into the folds of her scarf and slowly settles her weary, down-cocooned body to doze in the protective skidoo. She is unimpressed by any sibling's prowess at mastery of the side step. The outsize sun glasses stay firmly attached to the face above the pink nose, and the ski-hat bobble rolls into a fold made by the child's all-consuming fleece blanket. To a caring onlooker, the child might have expired. The mother isn't worried; this is a way of life in the snow. She cuddles Nicholas, congratulates him on his side-stepping skills, and collects miniature skis and *batons* into a sack on her back. All three slowly drift away, their breath condensing in wispy clouds in the early evening air, the skidoo gliding across perfect *piste*.

The 'newborn' is cosy and fast asleep, totally unaware of her side-stepping potential and that she might, one day, represent her nation on the snow.

This is how France 'grows' her ski champions.

CHANCE ENCOUNTER IN FRANCE

It bared its teeth. It clenched its jaw;
the creature from the second floor.
From nostrils flared, green snot ran down
beneath slit eyes and fuming frown.
It seized its chance. She'd let it loose;
the monster with the missing tooth.
It trailed a doll impaled with pins.
I felt a chill swirl round my shins.
It balled a fist, its digits curled.
Could this vile *it* be of our world?
I smiled 'Bonjour'. I know it heard,
but it slunk past without a word.
It picked its nose, then scratched its bum.
It yawned a lot then sucked its thumb.
It sat down, shrieked (just like my cat);
not four years old in bobble hat.
Its mother sighed, stubbed out her fag
and tore downstairs with filthy rag.
She wiped its nose and boxed its ears.
The monster yelled and shed more tears.
The mother tied it to her broom
and flew the warlock to his room,
where spells and curses filled the air.
To mention more, I wouldn't dare.
I gave the boy the widest berth;
still questioned if he's of this earth.
I stuck a doll, ripped up a hen.
I never saw the child again.

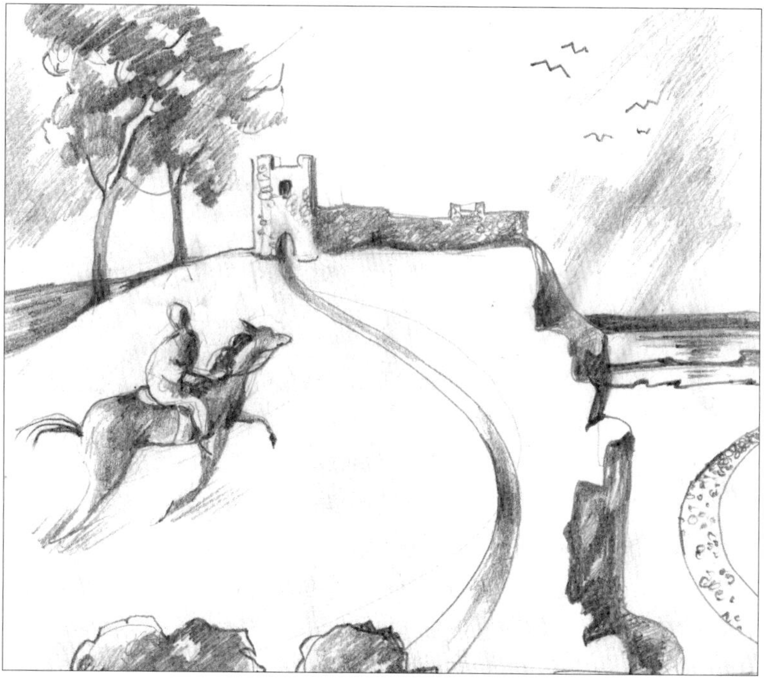

HUNTING THE WORM FROM PENNARD CASTLE

In vivid dreams, my caparisoned mare
prances, nostrils flaring, scenting the chase.
We leave the postern gate and cross the links
where men will swing their clubs, not in battle,
centuries after our keep is fragments;
where haunting vassal souls speak in whispers.

My squire confirms a sighting and whispers,
around first light, that faithful men, and mare,
are keen to hunt. He speaks of charred fragments,
uprooted saplings. The cwm's woodland chase
has been scorched, as though a mighty battle
has raged. We don mail, securing the links.

It is clear the forest damage has links
with the creature we seek. There are whispers
that others, Kittle folk, have seen battle
but none returned except a distressed mare,
which lackeys tried to sooth after a chase
by the shore; its harness blackened fragments.

My men hold fast, until the sun fragments
behind smoke drifting down the pill. Firm links
established now, we urge our mounts to chase
across water, sand, silt, scrub. Faint whispers
reach our ears from far out west. My brave mare
surges forward to engage in battle.

The clifftops are parched; black. My men battle
through dark, sulphurous clouds, scattered fragments
of pigs, cows, sheep consumed by fire. A mare,
loose, whinnies pain. Undeniable links
beckon toward land's end. The sea whispers,
then steams, as the evil worm cedes the chase.

The worm drowns; a fitting end to our chase.
We, with no recourse to sword or battle,
rejoice that the scourge is dead. The whispers
circulate; our tale of valour fragments
as centuries pass and dubious links
tell of Pennard's Lord and his fearless mare.

The faithful mare and the story's fragments
lie scattered on links where men do battle.
Ghostly whispers relate the dragon chase.

INSIDE OUT

Goliath's double built our flat-pack tank
and left us inside, out among the shrubs.
We had majestic dreams; stretched canvas blank.
We'd not allowed for spiders, flies or grubs
which love the heat a five-blade fan churns round.
Sky speeds above; time-lapse we can't rewind.
The constellations glint, like treasures drowned
in water dyed deep blue where light is shined.
We steam in sunshine: heat enough to singe.
Wet laundry dries on dreary afternoons.
Surf sails twink like tight-shut butterfly wings.
Kites soar, tugging on anchors in the dunes.
The cherished light around us is the prize,
and seeing nature blossom through tired eyes.

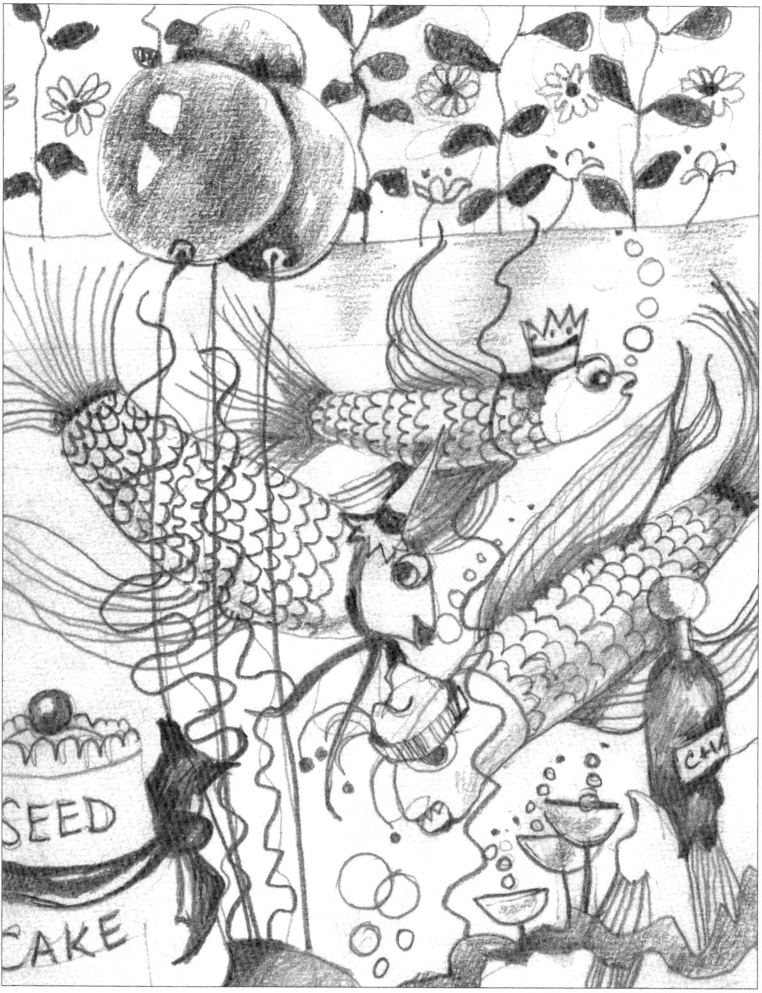
SEED
CAKE
CHA

SYNCHRONY INSPIRED BY A NEW TANK
(After James Tate's 'Consolations After an Affair')

My shubunkins now swim in tight formation;
they are organising a gala
on Friday next week, strictly before feeding time.

(There are stuffed trophies on shelves
that dream they still roam free the Serengeti.
They knew the hunting tactics of fellow creatures.
An impala would not linger, at dusk,
by a lonely water hole.)

I've mentioned I approached the Bank
for a loan to replace their present tank.

My blue Persian purrs beside me;
a distant dial-tone.
And she aches for the fresh taste of gold fish
who'll brag their new element.

THE GARDEN ANGEL
*(Dedicated to Michael Johnson, Resident Harpist,
Melbourne Royal Botanic Gardens, June 2008)*

Not hewn stone,
lovingly
his fingers
caress strings.
Melodies
dance through glades;
by a lake thronged
with floating
listeners.

Not cast bronze,
tenderly
his body
bends; senses
rhythmical
cadences
through the frame
beneath his
strong shoulder.

Not thrown clay,
thoughtfully
his gracious
countenance
moves to the
sforzandi

or the calm
lullaby,
eyes closed wide.

Enchanted
toddlers twirl,
heads giddy,
to the tunes.
Clapping hands
complement
fluttering
of shy fowl
in thickets.

We land-bound
gardeners
pause awhile,
admiring
his singing
harp. We smile,
turn faces
to the sun,
or staunch tears.

THE LEAVING

I'm leaving home with my Teddy tonight.
(The weatherman promised the moon will be bright
so I'll not need a torch, and I know where to go.
I'll leave not a trace in the new-fallen snow.)
We've argued enough about *carrots and greens*
and I won't tolerate any more angry scenes
about sizes of helpings and how to 'Set to!'
when they're both served up with dumplings and stew.

I'm leaving home with my Teddy tonight.
(I thought I might tell you, but knew you'd take fright.
So, I'm scribbling this note. There's no cause for alarm.
I'll take care of myself. I'll come to no harm.)
I'm going to hide on my own. I've a bed
on the cold wooden floor in an old garden shed.
And I won't need to slave at keeping it neat,
or change the socks on my flat, stinky feet.

I'm leaving home with my Teddy tonight.
(The chance that you'll miss me by morning is slight.
So you'll doubtless rush round, like a demented fool,
shrieking ten times or more that 'we'll be late for school!)
The clothes I've got on will last me for years
and I'm not going to bother cleaning my ears,
or washing my hair, or scrubbing my neck.
I've reached the stage where I think 'Oh, what the heck!'

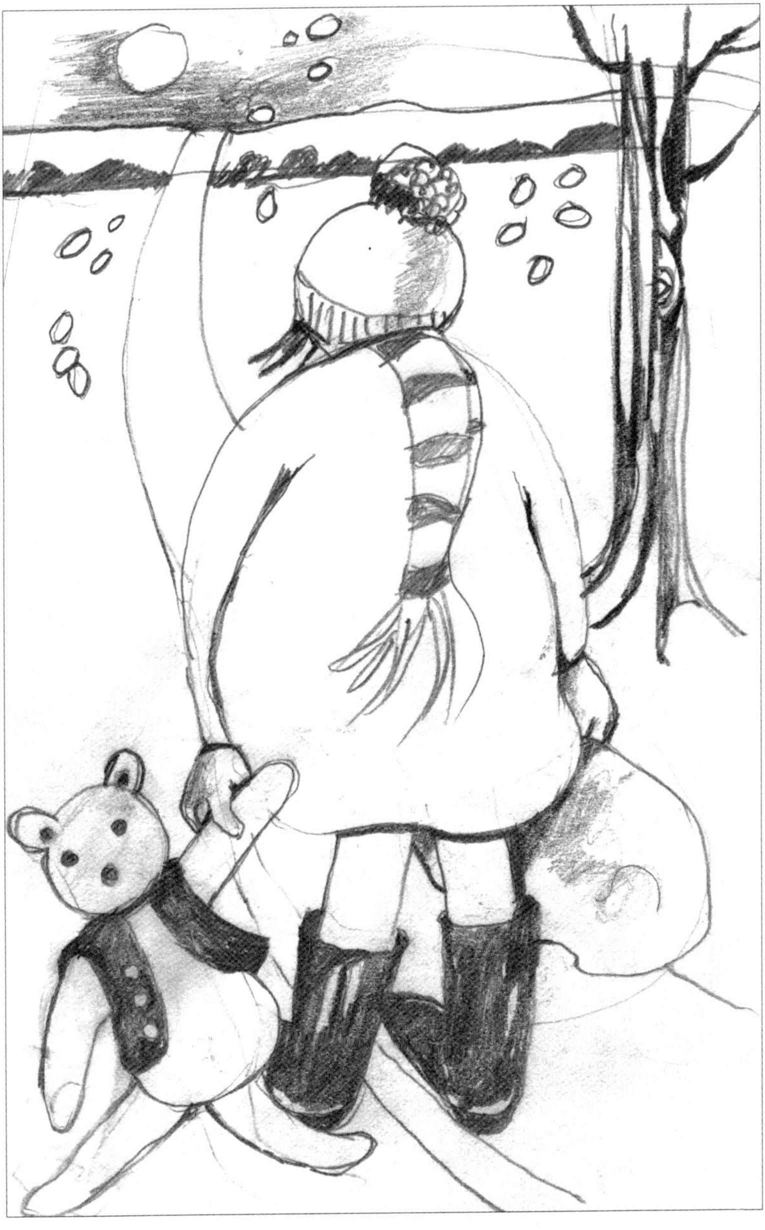

I'm leaving home with my Teddy tonight.
(The thought of my plan fills me with delight.
I've packed all my things in an old threadbare sheet
and I'll set off quite soon when the snow turns to sleet.)
You'll be glad when I've gone; there'll be no need to shout,
or frown, nag or snort or tear your hair out.
The house will be quiet, dreary and sad
without me. You'll have time to talk lots with Dad.

I'm leaving home with my Teddy right now.
(Not thought about food, but I'll manage somehow
on a cucumber sandwich, a jar of Marmite
and a bottle of pop for a feast at midnight.)
Then I'll snuff out my candle and settle to doze
and hope I don't suffer frostbite in my toes.
I've got the *best* pillow, my furry Ted's tummy.
God bless, and don't worry about me. Yours, Mummy.

JOURNEY

Circle Line. Saturday morning.
Underground, as day just dawning.

Obese woman, cheeks a-glowing,
flops down, backside over-flowing.

Brassy bimbo, both breasts thrusting.
White stick. Blind man, guide dog trusting.

Through dark tunnels, couplings rattling.
Wakeful toddler, loudly prattling.

Gent in dress suit, head bowed dozing,
starts at message 'doors are closing'.

White skins, black, pale, tanned or peeling.
Eyes averted study the ceiling,
or tick off stops on the route marked yellow.

High Street Ken. On climbs a fellow.
Chats up bimbo, strong hands groping.
She's ecstatic; spent all year hoping.

Dowdy spinster, spectacles shining,
imagines romance for which she's pining.

Pasty faces. Jaws wide yawning.
Circle Line. Saturday morning.

THE COCKFOSTERS TERRORISTS
(For Doreen & Chloe)

Piccadilly Line on amber alert,
today, between Cockfosters and Bounds Green.

Cool guy – denims, rugged – began to flirt;
eyelashes longer than any I'd seen
on a male, equivalent to plumage
proffered by cock to peahen. Some bonus!

So, I'm entranced by being centre stage,
but not so's not to notice panic as
two puffed-up pigeons swagger, flap; distraught
to find themselves on the ten-forty-two
heading for Heathrow. And they won't be caught.
The flirt's too scared. (I'll bet his name is Hugh.)

Folks cover heads with papers, bags. They scream.
The pigeons 'mind the gap', alight, then preen.

TO THE BETTER END

You sleep all night doing it.
You spend the day ruing it;
snoring, that is.

You spend the money, burning it,
while I'm on duty earning it;
wages, I mean.

You can't be bothered cooking stuff
and leave the house to gather fluff.
Lazy, I think.

You find it hard to multi-task,
not hearing questions when I ask.
Are you deaf, too?

You've little taste for upbeat style;
refuse with patronizing smile.
Agree! It's true!

You're selfish, boring, past your best.
I need to get this off my chest.
Finished, aren't we?

You were my lover and best friend,
but now I want a better end:
distance between.
You make a list, divide our home,
except I claim the garden gnome
for pastures fresh.

You'll find another bloke to love
and settle down like hand in glove.
You'll feel brand new.

SEASCAPE CHARACTERS – OXWICH BEACH

Their black silhouettes contrast starkly against the autumnal blandness of the Oxwich seashore.

Not difficult to notice, the two of them would normally blend anonymously into a mid-summer throng of beach lovers. Now, like overfed Lowry characters they interrupt the empty horizon, drawing my attention to their aloneness together.

They may have bought identical single-breasted mackintoshes in a job-lot sale. I can imagine them auditioning successfully for parts as Mr and Mrs Noah in an am dram festival epic. Except that I expect the biblical Mr Noah did not dream of taking a paddle when the rains began to pour on his handiwork.

Midday; above the tide-darkened, soggy sand, the drizzle has ceased. Mrs Noah stands immovable, stoic, watching her animated companion bend to hoist his grey flannels knee-wards. As he struggles, he totters, almost toppling forward into the wavelets drowning his paper-pale, thin ankles.

What passion drives him deeper into the oncoming tide, gingerly arching his feet and legs above each roll of white foam threatening to engulf the concertinaed trouser legs?

Mrs Noah, heart in mouth, and certainly not relishing the threat of damp and smelly woollen slacks on the return car journey, averts her gaze and turns away, to avoid the inevitable. Mr Noah pits his tiptoe potential against shifting, tide-washed, sand ripples now thirty centimetres below rising high water.

She cannot watch. It is all too much to bear and goodness knows what other spectators might think.

Yes, here I am. I can see you both. I, too, am fearful for cramped, cold calves, and wonder how Mrs Noah's wrath will descend on Mr Noah. Will you be a nagging wife wailing like a siren in the mist, or will you admonish the wayward, childlike wanderer with a clip around his ear?

With a bodily sigh, she turns, and moves up the beach, not wishing to be seen one part of the pair.

Mr Noah wades on with aplomb, and elemental expertise.

WORKOUT WORSHIP
(After Sir John Betjeman's 'A Subaltern's Love-song')

Miss Charlotte Sims-Green, Miss Charlotte Sims-Green,
(tattooed, toned totty – the fittest I've seen)
those extended lunges you make me perform
have toned my limp limbs, though I'm knackered and worn.

I sing to your music; rapt by your words,
I'm not put off by the other plump birds
posturing, galloping, stretching *en masse*,
and I love being ordered, '*Let's kick some ass!*'

Miss Charlotte Sims-Green, Miss Charlotte Sims-Green,
I've come to you, eager to lose weight, look lean.
My Nikes are on order, I've wristbands in plum,
and my mauve Primark hoodie disguises my bum.

The weight I've been bearing will drop off, I'm sure.
I've more than blind faith in your aerobic cure.
I'll go through the motions, at home, before sleep,
then stretch out, relax, and ensure I breathe deep.

The cost of your sessions, the post-workout swims,
the latte and waffles we scoff at *Slim Jim*'s,
the facials, pedicures, manicures, saunas,
are steadily putting points on my corners.

On the desk in my study, I've photos that show
the way I once looked. Now, my envied pink glow,
which stems from endorphins and feeling the burn,
is what girlfriends remark upon; makes heads turn.

My motorbike's revving in tandem with yours.
I spend *all* my leisure time, now, out of doors,
adoring the mud, slime, showers, storms, sun,
and your lithe, perfect, outline – second to none.

Your leathers are racy, your sleepers pure gold.
You're classy and sassy. Your smile's never cold,
and I long to kiss its thin moon crescent,
but there's never a time when others aren't present.

Miss Charlie Sims-Green, Miss Charlie Sims-Green,
your chrome ghetto-blaster's working up steam
and you're bending, plié-ing, pliant; like down
from a snow-goose a soft breeze has blown.

About me are tubbies and fatties; a score.
Before me, you – Charlie – the girl I adore.
I want to know, what is the secret you keep?
Do you work out, post-midnight, while we're asleep?

I've sworn to the others, I'll keep watch one night
when classes have closed and the moon's beaming bright.
I'll tail you, take notes and report back. I'm keen
to learn all about gorgeous Charlotte Sims-Green.

A BUMP ON THE HEAD

Let this story be a warning to all unsuspecting wives, especially those post-menopausal tubbies who rest upon their laurels after more than forty years of being spliced to handsome, wayward hubbies.

He'll hint broadly that the house should have a *facelift before long*; that he'll happily fill hairline cracks with plaster, whilst you sugar-soap the paintwork and wild-daffodil the walls because, you're *good at it – you'll work much faster*.

So you set to, one fine morning, with the vacuum and brute force, whilst he swans off to his Club for golf then dinner. At least, that's where you think he is – and you feel quite chuffed that, come tomorrow, both of you might well look thinner.

When you've finished sweeping down every ceiling, wall, and lintel, he'll whisk round, in flannels, plugging gaps with filler. You'll think it strange you're clothed in tat whilst he is looking smart, oblivious that he's wondering *Could I kill her?*

Cos for ages he's been playing Sugar Daddy to a woman who's young – a Geordie, single – and she's skinny. She loves his looks, his waist, his thighs (his balding bits are few) and he can't resist her when she whispers *hinny*. So, you persevere, climb ladders, wield the roller 'til it hurts whilst he plots an artful cast-iron alibi. He'll blame your death on vertigo, and being rather weighty. The coroner's verdict – *Death by DIY*!

Let my story be a warning to you single-minded wives, whose decorating skills make houses cleaner. This fatal bump upon my head has not been caused by toppling. Len's hammer fell because I was not leaner.

ALPHABET OF SUMMER 2003 EXPANSION

Ably assisted in April by an
abundantly dry atmosphere,
builders brought their bums to the Bay,
braving breezes, where boxers or
briefs fell well
below belt and –
boringly –
just above bronzed buttocks.

Carefully they cracked open its
coating and
carted the concrete carapace of our
casa to a container
designed to deal with the
disposal of dross.

Eagerly, we energized each morning,
expecting our efficient engineers to emerge
from their Foden Freeloader
full of the frolics of this
fine late spring.

Generally, the guys greeted us gladly, but
gave little ground about
holidays, hang-gliding, hitchhiking, or other
hobbies they hankered for.

Inhalation interludes were
intermittent and
inoffensive.
Juggling judiciously, in
jaunty jumpers stamped with surfing motifs, they
jumped about with heavy tools on scaffolding.

Keen as kippers, to
kit us out with
king-size pins to
keep the house from
keeling over, they
Kango'd the kitchen wall, sometimes
kneeling in the rubble.

Later, when the house
looked lamentably lopsided without its
liberal layer of light-coloured chippings, they
managed to manufacture a marvellous new
main entrance
made of armoured UPVC, with
mastic manoeuvred into the
many gaps.
Needless to say, perhaps, we
now have a neat,
north-facing n-trance. This
opens into elements which only occasionally
overwhelm us as an
occlusion settles directly
overhead.

Plaster was pertly
put in place by the Master and his pal and
parallel lines were picked out of it to
provide the perfect key for a
quagmire of quick-setting concrete onto which
rained pebbles at a rollicking rate to
render and reinforce our
renovations.

Sun shone down on scaffolding,
scanty in places (which was a bit of a
shock to the squad, who

selected spots to schedule the work
so that they didn't
slide off.)

Tiffin times were tenfold
throughout the team's working day.
Tea and occasional teacakes, taken
together on the top terrace,
usually urged the builders into
unburdening themselves about
ulcers, ukulele playing (an unusual pastime)
umpires at umpteen Rugby
Union matches, undertaking and
underwear!

Varieties of the latter were vigorously vaunted:
vanilla-scented, varicoloured. Even
vegetarian velveteen is available, they verified.
Wondering, this week,
why in the world
workmen would want to wear
xmas-tree Xeroxed
ylang ylang-scented
Y-fronts, which have to be
yanked over the yawning,
zig-zagging, lumbar zone, with
zeal and zest, I
zero in on

an active assessment of the
attractiveness or abomination of last
April, when
builders brought their
bums to the Bay.

Oh, hell! – Must call it a day . . .

HOW TO BE A WRITER

You need a good pen.
You need a fat pad.
You need to have lived through good times and bad.
You need keen eyes.
You need clean ears
to listen to folks who speak of their fears.

Your spelling and grammar can be shot to hell
as long as you've a good yarn to tell
and folks understand the words that you mean.
You must have talent to picture a scene,
or several; depends on the project you've chosen.
You'll write winter stuff, on location, hands frozen.

You'll write in your bed.
You'll write on the train
'til your writing flows like a flood down a drain.

You must write every day,
even if it's email.
You don't know what might end up in a tale
of romance, or intrigue, or a family drama.
If you get writer's block, wait a day 'til you're calmer.

Collect lists of similes, metaphors, 'handles'
and pre-empt power cuts with loads of fat candles.
You should find that, with time, your writing gets better,
and you may just feel brave about sending a letter
to an agent or publisher keen to agree
to promote your work for a modest (fat?) fee.
But until that day dawns, keep your work neatly stored.
When you know you're a writer, you'll never be bored.

PRETENDING
(For Watercolour Society of Wales artist, Janet Weeks Bligh)

Strolling down Pobbles' marram-matted dune
he reaches the strand; deserted, wild, drowned
by a mid-autumn spring tossing its spume
beyond stones, shells, flotsam marooned aground.

A staff – heartwood fissured, scoured of its bark –
lies bleached.
Goliath's shin-bone washed ashore?
Or Tolkien's wizard-wand – its magic mark
abhorred by evil creatures of Mordor?

He clasps this stout stick, challenging the tide;
King Canute.
Arms spread wide, he summons cloud,
lightning, thunder, gale!

With no place to hide
on that stricken shore,
soaked through, chilled and cowed,
he stabs the staff, upright, into firm sand;
leaves it for the next unsuspecting hand.

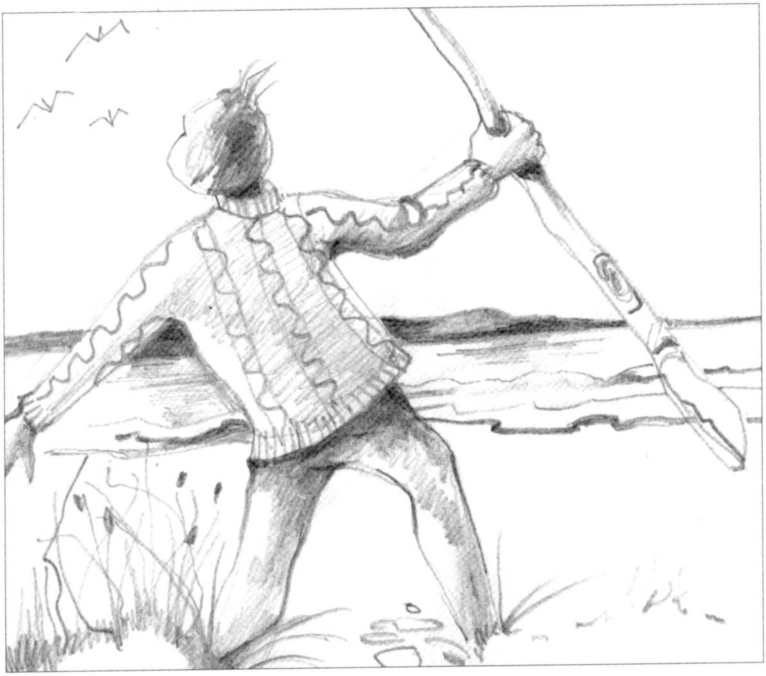

CLIFF-TOP TREES

Leaning, like drunks turning out after '*Time*',
arms tangled – as though each longs not to part
from buddies they've known through deep winter's rime,
spring blossoms, barleycorn cut for the cart –
their gnarled-bark skeletons slant to the lea,
moulded since seedlings by gales from out west;
withstanding buffeting winds off rough sea
rampaging through limestone slades. Just one nest –
home to blackbird broods, delicately built
of moss, hair, twigs, twined to cup precious young –
rides out storms; a sail-free yacht at full tilt
holds fast its course in the bole where it's slung.
Sentinel silhouettes blown by the breeze
rarely grow lofty: staunch, squat, cliff-top trees.

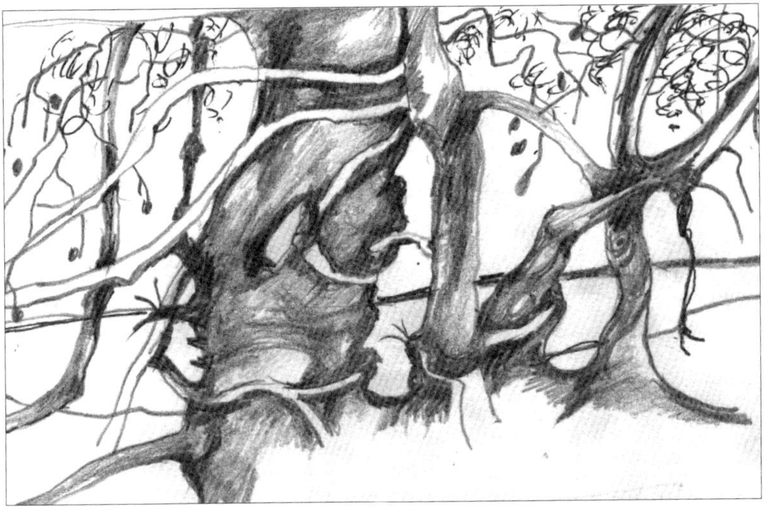

DROPPING ONE DIMENSION
*(After a presentation at Horton Village Hall
by Peter Nicholas, sculptor & artist, February 2011)*

The sculptor lays his lines on white support.
No pre-determined form flows from his hand;
these trails explore his lobes. Giving scant thought
to outcome, colours random, marks unplanned
map deserts, oceans, peaks: cross the frontier
between my bland and his mysterious.
Shades deepen, blooms flourish. Creatures appear
from the wild melange of deft, generous
brushstrokes clinging to contours. Emerald,
terra cotta, cobalt; earth's boundless hues.
His sable caresses each dip, curl, fold,
of this loose mindscape. Images confuse.
I strive to make some sense; to read his signs.
But fail to understand the sculptor's lines.

ONE PINK DIANTHUS
(Inspired by a portrait)

There are frustrating days, when it is just impossible to maintain the relentless composure demanded by the little Pisan painter. (I had no idea a detailed likeness, on a support of such small dimensions, would require so many laborious sittings!)

I wonder if he is far more confident of the end result than he would care to admit, and is taking advantage of me sitting here, sitting still, sitting in next-to-nothing, showing more than just my aristocratic profile. Leonello insists I be patient, co-operative, so that the portrait will be finished well before my time; that Pisanello has many commissions and will need to concentrate on those, as well as this image of me; will need to be away from Mantua for long intervals.

Some days are severely itchy, in the early and mid-summer, when the mosquitoes are inquisitive, insistent, intolerable. Why cannot they hover and pester directly along the banks of the Mincio? Why must they invade the Castello? When they swarm and inevitably land in the wet tempera, Antonio pokes his brush onto their bodies and loads more colour where they've paddled on the wood's surface. He tells me he is unconcerned when the insects avoid my likeness and stamp over the painting's background. He tells me he will be most concerned if one of the vile creatures punctures my smooth, pale flesh and I succumb to the horror the flies carry from Lake Garda. Already this year, the builders have been badly stricken. Their labours on San Giorgio have been interrupted, whilst men sweat and shake through the sickness for which the apothecary offers little comfort. We try, as much as possible, to avoid direct contact with any servants.

There are steamy days, when I must pose motionless in my cool linen chemise whilst Antonio concentrates, for hours at a time, on my features. He has made no reference to, or decision about, my raiment for the final sitting. But he has explained to me his vision which demands – and will complement – the denial of my crowning glory. As befits my newly-married status, my hair shall be braided and bound in a matron's cap, to enhance the elegance of my noble neck. Would that it did not ache so, as he constantly reminds me to sit still! It is hard for me to remain calm, when he speaks of Verona or Rome; paints pictures on my mind of grandeur in those cities I have not seen which are many days' ride distant.

'You should come to my home, Pisa, one day, Margherita; perhaps in spring next year, when the flies are not such a problem.'

'What will interest me there?' I ask, longing to turn my head to speak directly to Pisanello. He sighs and continues to dab at the panel. He is not satisfied with the pigment he has chosen for my flesh tones. He answers quietly, slowly.

'The Campanile is an amusement; such folly to have built, with costly marble, on such an insecure site. Here we are, over two-and-a-half centuries later, and the bell tower continues to lean. An inebriated strumpet in a white nightgown has a greater chance of remaining attractive, functional and upright if her feet are firmly anchored to the ground. I think perhaps the Campanile might lean too far and collapse before long . . . Yes, you must come see this shining treasure before it is too late. The leaning tower is very beautiful, my dear – but not as beautiful as you, Margherita de Gonzaga.'

He studies me for a long time, nodding his head in agreement with his own suggestion, and then returns his piercing gaze to concentrate further on my profile. He demands the same accuracy for this painting as he uses for the medals he's creating of our great ducal leaders of Italy.

There are cool days endured in the salon close by the braziers. The Castello can be bitterly cold. The damp penetrates the very walls. I have furs to sit upon, to protect me from the draughts created by busy servants, who are often a distraction to me. They beg leave to continue with their duties, which is granted by us both. But I notice a distinct tardiness about their tasks as they gawp at the majesty of this live exhibit, about whom they will perhaps tell their children, 'I was in service in '36, just before she grew too wide for the picture frame.'

On occasions, Pisanello chats to me about his plans for the all-important background to my portrait. Leonello demands of him that nothing should detract from my radiant splendour; that perhaps the scene should be quite bland, finished in one of the paler shades of the d'Este family crest. But I am certain Antonio has other ideas. Before securing this commission from my father, the Pisan proudly displayed his many preliminary animal sketches, showing unrivalled fine detail, indicative of the infinite care he takes in draughtsmanship. But, since approving his initial drafts, after the introductory meeting last spring, new sketchbooks are brought to us bursting with blooms, buds, leaves, tendrils, stamens, and life-like butterfly forms which seem to flutter above the parchment. Antonio is of a mind to scatter random blooms against a bosky background; has suggested I consider columbines and dianthus attracting swallowtails and admirals. My feeling – and I've given this a good deal of thought – is that perhaps one or two pink dianthus would not outshine my countenance. Antonio is anxious to create added interest in this portrait for our family collection. So, who am I to argue? The artist knows best. He will please Leonello and that will be an end to it.

Now, once more, mid-summer's day approaches. Most of the men and stable-boys have joined the riding party. Their departure has left the Castello unusually quiet. They hunt somewhere south of the city. Rumour has it that deer are plentiful and in need of the Mincio's cool shallows. We shall likely feast well, for many weeks, when their catch is hauled back.

It is far too hot, but today I don my gown and robe so that pigment comparisons can be made, to best capture the bodice's silk threads and the translucency of the seed pearls adorning my sleeves. The clothes are cumbersome but regal, as befits the status of the Gonzaga and d'Este dynasties.

I am perspiring, but wine is on hand and I drink at every opportunity when Antonio allows me to relax. He has tweaked a juniper cutting from the formal hedge in the piazza. I wear the sprig above my left armpit, where the seamstress has not performed to her usual standard. (If her eyesight isn't failing, she will be suitably admonished!) The juniper twig is dark, fresh and full. I breathe in the bitter-sweet aroma.

The Pisan forbids me to smile, so my jaws are clenched. My expression must show passive acceptance and patience in this first pregnancy. Of course, when the project started all those months ago, I was not to know a child would slightly complicate matters. This gown is so very heavy today but, mercifully, hides the quickened offspring.

I look the maiden, still. If I could let down my hair, Antonio would surely have a challenge on his hands!

The salon is stifling, with little air to relieve us. The child pounds its feet against my ribcage.

My chemise is not as tidily tucked in as my tresses. This matron's cap is altogether unbecoming. I am flustered and feeling faint. My eyes are heavy. I could sleep right here and now. I have had enough of posturing and posing for my husband's pleasure.

I stare into nothingness and ponder upon how the revered Antonio Pisanello will complete his portrayal of Margherita de Gonzaga in this year of Our Lord, fourteen hundred and thirty-seven. I am fortunate to be sitting for an artist who is recognised as an unsurpassed painter of the natural world, but I fear that too many random botanical images will detract from my delicate beauty.

One pink dianthus – a blossom symbol of the love and fertility I share with my darling Leonello – might have taken the place of this snatched juniper twig. Pisanello says he has included the juniper, because it foretells the birth of a male child. Leonello will be delighted at the prediction.

But it is now too late to argue about the portrait's background. Antonio tells me he is finally inspired; that the portrait will be delivered in twenty more days. I shall be immortalised, for as long as the wood on which I'm painted survives. Our children will be able to gaze upon their mother's dazzling loveliness long after her graceful body putrefies beneath the sod.

As Pisanello's work for our family finishes, it will not be long before mine begins in earnest. I have been pampered these long months and need to direct my thoughts to the care of Leonello's child; sew fine swaddling for him.

I wait expectantly, with the infinite patience of the newly-portrayed.

STOUTHALL BUTTERCUPS

We sauntered
lightly as two clouds that drift
o'er flocks of ewes and tups.
Then, fleet of foot,
in dew-filled grass,
we trampled golden buttercups.

THE SOLICITOUS LIMPET

She thought she heard a limpet sigh!
Spring sun shone warm; deep blue the sky.
No breeze disturbed the seashore pool.
She held her breath; felt such a fool.

The rocks were dry; the tide was out.
Perhaps the limpet meant to shout
a warning to the limpet crowd
to cling on tight. Its sigh was loud.

She stood stock-still; scanned Horton's rocks.
The seashore pool washed round her socks,
as sand gave way beneath her feet.
She swore her heart had missed a beat.

She climbed those rocks to firmer ground,
and sat awhile, without a sound,
unsure quite what she hoped to find.
(Do languid molluscs speak their mind?)

She thought she heard a limpet sigh,
and vowed that she would stay close by
that rock, from which the plaintive groan
enthralled her as she strolled alone.

By now, the tide was on the turn.
Her knees and feet began to burn.
She watched the limpets carefully,
as water rose relentlessly.

The limpet shells clung hard and fast,
relieved to be submerged at last
uncrushed; surviving one more tide.
She suddenly felt sick inside.

The tidal race flowed strong and deep.
All she could do was try to keep
herself from sinking more and more.
She tried, in vain, to reach the shore.

And just before she drowned that day,
she realised, with grave dismay,
she *had* heard that limpet shout,
to warn her she was too far out.

The Solicitous Limpet
(Image courtesy of J. Winder)

Rochers de Fiz, Plate Massif, Haut Savoie

SIXTY

Shrinking stature,
size susceptible, my
skin slackens and
slides, surely,
stain-spotted,
south.

Sloping eyelids,
sagging jowls,
smiles of a lifetime
streaked scars by
sliver-lipped
mouth.

Sport-stressed spine
screams during slumber.
Sleep beyond seven's –
same as sex – a
sensation from a
sun-drenched
youth.

THE TEST OF TIME

I must go down to the sea again for a '99' cone in the sun, and a browse in the shop with the kiss-me-quick hats; it's years since I bought myself one.

I must walk barefoot on the beach at least once with a bucket, a spade and a net, and I'll welcome the splash of the waves on my toes. I just hope I don't get my clothes wet.

I might book a trip on an open-topped bus to relive childhood memories again. But I'll take my blue brolly, just in case, as the forecast is threatening rain.

I might sample winkles, cockles and eels – a few moules, too – I won't go without. And with some good luck, if it's opening time, I can guzzle a pint of milk stout.

I must visit the funfair, take aim at some ducks, have my palm read by Gypsy Rose Scroggins, ride a carousel horse, eat some pink candy floss, wash it down with two more milk stout noggins.

I might pose for a snap in the booth on the pier, where my face will complete a cartoon. Then I'll amble along in the afternoon breeze, fist clutching a large red balloon.

I may trek to the lighthouse (which now has no keeper –
he retired and has since bought a dog). The light's automatic.
It shines all night long. The horn booms at the first hint of fog.

I may wander along to the bandstand; on Sunday the 'Army' is playing. I'll join in with community singing, but have second thoughts about praying.

Then I'll think about leaving the coast for my home, quite drained from this week's hectic test to challenge the theory some people expound that a change is as good as a rest!

ON GETTING ON, NOT GETTING OFF

The beauty mags tell women, on almost every page, about the tricks to hold at bay the rigours of old age. With creams to firm up buttocks and toxin for thin lips, I could become the modern 'face to launch a thousand ships'.

Why don't I look like Fonda? I worked out – *burned* – for years, but all I have to show for that are dainty, once-pierced ears. I've eyelids short of lashes and irises mouse-brown. The furrowed trenches through my brow disclose how much I frown.

My laughter lines are showing. My smile lifts cheeks grown slack and camouflages constant pain I suffer with my back. My feet are worn from walking – too far. I've toes like claws, and rather than wear sexy thongs, my bum fits best in drawers which cover every dimple from armpits down to crutch. No VPL's revealed behind. (You see, I'm still *in touch!*).

But what's out front's alarming. I've tyres which don't deflate. I measure almost size sixteen. What happened to size eight, when legs were made for 'minis' and t-shirts hugged 'blue eyes'? It's decades, physiology, and eating home-baked pies.

My moles have finished digging. They bloom in awkward clumps, and recently my finger-joints have sprouted clicking bumps.

I've come to a conclusion and given up on men. With thinning hair and clapped-out knees, I need to think again. Will my pension stretch to buy a set of smart false teeth, and though I dress up like a lamb, will mutton show beneath?

I'm working on my problems. I rise at dawn each day and flick through all the magazines that have too much to say on cellulite, and mauve thread veins, and why one's hair turns white, decreased libido, HRT, incontinence, short-sight.

This getting-on's a bugger. What can I do but stride? I'm thankful that my brain's alert. The same young chick's inside.

TOAD IN THE HOLE

I
thought of
knocking up couscous
in a traditional tagine,
then thought tiffin should be
baked beans, toad in the hole,
buttered-mashed-crème-fraiched, grill-seared Desiree.
Blowout – Yorkshire pudding billowing like *Cutty Sark*'s sails!

LOOKING BACK – SEPTEMBER 2003

Looking back,
I intended to capture you;
stop time's march
for just one reason.
No maudlin premeditation, this.
Just some lines, (*Ecclesiasticals*! – you would joke)
'to everything there is a season . . .'
shrieked at me.
You posed regally,
the shutter snapped,
and I captured you.

The sun shone
in the instant I hoarded you;
your profile
bold on bright backdrop.
A classic, quick, composition, this.
Pose good, (*This view's fantastical*! – fixed on grin)
'a time to every purpose under heaven . . .'
weighed me down.
I feared, needlessly.
The shutter snapped
and I understood.

With hindsight,
I needed to embrace your soul
last springtime
in landscape you loved.
No shallow self-deception in this.
You were sure. (*Indefatigable's how I feel!*)
'A time to be born, and a time to die . . .'
soothes our days.
You knew all too well.
The shutter snapped
and saved your brave face.

ALL PRESENT AND CORRECT

After months of nagging at us, finally, Mum's home; technically, repatriated. I'm sure she's going to be content. If ever you'd heard her denouncing the principality and its natives – *though she married a Welsh-born soldier, endured his Llanstephan-loving mother, and spent countless summer holidays on Carmarthenshire sands* – you'd understand the recriminations we've tolerated these past three years. But today we're back on Essex soil. The old girl's where she belongs, though she wouldn't recognise the Southend-on-Sea she saw through child's eyes.

The tide's way out. The town's untidily off-season. Sharp, overnight frost defies weak sunshine, which hasn't penetrated the grey, pre-noon mist. Our breath condenses in it; disperses like wraiths flitting through the Memorial Garden. The timing's slightly inconvenient for us both, just three weeks before Christmas, but was dictated by blighted local government bureaucracy. It's taken us almost two months to get this far. All would have been unnecessary if we'd decided Mum should stay near us, over the border in what she termed 'the wilds'. But I couldn't bear the thought that, if our house sale went through, we'd be abandoning Mum for ever. After my sensitive suggestion, and following through on the required research, we're going for this with clear consciences. The plan's one she'd never have conceived over tea and digestives. And we're granting Mum's wishes too.

She could rarely be bothered to make any decisions. For the past thirty-five years, she just wanted to die. *What a way to live a life!*

Janice, at The Sutton Road Lodge, answered Tony's enquiry, sounding as though she'd been in service since the cemetery opened in nineteen hundred.

'Good day to you, and how may I assist?'

'It's about a family burial plot. My father paid a fee for it in nineteen forty-five. The name's Dobbs – D. O. B. B. S. My parents' first-born baby was buried there in the September. I've a certificate if that'll help.'

'Name?' asked Janice.

'Barry Christopher Dobbs – D. O. B. B. S.'

'Barry Christopher. Buried here in nineteen forty-five? If that's so, then the plot will have reverted in nineteen ninety-five; after fifty years we recycle the ground again, you see. What's the reason for your enquiry?'

'Well, I'm hoping to re-unite my mother with her child. I wonder whether Mum's ashes might be interred at Sutton Road in the family plot.'

'Did your mother record her wishes in her will?'

'No. I've made that decision for her, at my wife's suggestion. No-one else needs to be consulted. I'm her sole executor.'

'Is your father alive?' enquired Janice, to which Tony replied in the negative.

'Where is your father then? Did he not come here when he died, and why not?' *Weren't these questions above and beyond Janice's remit?*

'Dad was cremated in October, nineteen sixty-nine. Mum was too distraught then to consider doing anything which wasn't suggested by the undertakers. I think she just forgot the Sutton Road plot was waiting to swallow Dad whole.' Tony tried to appeal to Janice's lighter side.

'Yes, I see. Well, we can allow the interment, and possibly in the same reverted, now-vacant, plot. I'll send you the appropriate application form, which must be returned with relevant copies of your late mother's various certificates. I'll include our fees list. You should instruct us fully as to your specific requirements and I'll see to it that your mother's remains will be properly cared for.'

And with that Janice dismissed us. After a fortnight, all was scheduled.

We're here – the three of us – just before our eleven-thirty appointment. We're scouring the entrance driveway for a sign of my in-laws. They said they'll try to get here; not that Tony's sister's in a fit state to comprehend what's happening now, nor that what resembles a Party Seven beer barrel in the crook of Tony's elbow holds her mother's remains. The barrel's deep red.

There were only two colours available. Mum would've shuddered in her shroud at the thought of her ashes being shovelled into a bottle-green urn. She detested green. She'd donate green-tinted Christmas or birthday gifts: aprons, oven gloves, bath salts, soaps, stationery, headscarves. The local charity shop staff were genuinely thrilled to receive her contributions.

Mum couldn't abide shell pink either, but went to the flame cocooned in pink lawn, because we thought she'd look particularly washed-out in white. We had the choice of just the two colours. Recent legislation has denied folks a preferred funeral outfit, and Mum – unlike her best mate Doreen – hadn't specified what she'd prefer to wear, to go 'upstairs'. Doreen, who for years was fully prepared for death, had hung a slip, dress, jacket, laddered tights and a Pacamac on a hook behind her bedroom door, defying her minder to tidy them away. Mum's minder wouldn't even have looked behind the bedroom door! She rarely did anything more for Mum than brew a cuppa on her Monday-to-Friday daily visits. By the time Mum was taken into hospital for the last time, her once-pristine flat resembled a doss house. Mum never returned home. She came to us, on Gower, instead.

Tony shifts the urn into his other arm.

'They're not going to turn up, you know. Bloody typical! It's time. We'll have to get cracking, just the two of us.' And he shepherds me through The Lodge entrance into the furnace of the waiting room. Dove-grey Flotex complements the terracotta or grey adorning walls, skirting boards, and high-backed reclaimed church pews for weary backsides-in-waiting. A hatchway opens.

'Good morning and welcome. Are you the Dobbs family for eleven-thirty?' The receptionist beams at us from beneath a cropped bob. Her pose reminds me of La Gioconda. Tattered files overflow metal shelving behind her. On the counter, beneath the hatch, a poinsettia wilts in the dry heat. The woman – arms bare, plump, pink – has perhaps just suffered a menopausal flush. Her face is suffused with uneven red mottling; flesh resembling shins toasted too near an open fire.

'My name is Gwen. Gavin will conduct the ceremony for your late mother. Do you have your mother with you?' Gwen of the fixed grin gazes into the far distance, engaging directly with neither of us.

Tony deposits the Party Seven on the counter.

'Oh good,' says Gwen. 'Did you all have a good journey?' She opens a file containing our application forms, photocopies, and the cheque in settlement of the extortionate costs of today's outing; just under three hundred quid. 'Perhaps you weren't told when you made your original enquiry, but this local authority requires remains to be interred in metal rather than plastic. It's speedier biodegradability, you see. Gavin will transfer your mother to an appropriate casket, and then he'll proceed. It won't take two shakes. Do be seated and Gavin will join you shortly. I take it you don't wish to retain this container?' We decline. *What a ludicrous question!* Of course, Gwen's not to know the urn isn't a leftover from Mum's modest wake but an official one we collected from Morriston Crematorium eight weeks ago.

Gavin is a serious, lofty, round-shouldered young man with an obsequious expression. He'd make a fist of playing, to a tee, Uriah Heep in an am-dram 'Copperfield'. His black, woollen overcoat reaches to beneath his knees. The revers are black velvet. Gavin's hair is overlong and shiny. His shoes need some spit and polish. He sniffs every ten seconds or so.

'Dr Dobbs, sir, will you bear the urn to its final resting place?' asks Uriah, his eyelids a-flutter.

'No, Gavin, thanks. I'll let you do the honours.' *I know Tony wants to add, 'because we've paid eighty quid for you to lift it and hundreds more for the privilege of being here'.*

We solemnly process down Avenue 53, towards a square of ground devoid of monument or headstone. A freshly-excavated, giant molehill indicates what will be Mum's final resting place. I'm clutching Tony's arm, vaguely nervous now. Gavin's clutching Mum. We stop beside a hole in the ground. Our breath billows above our heads; even more hot air.

Gavin asks if Tony wishes to plant his Mum. Tony declines. So, Gavin does the honours. She'll be just two feet lower than ground level; not six under. *I must calculate the metric equivalent.*

'Do you both wish to say a prayer for the deceased? And, Dr Dobbs sir, do you wish to scatter some earth over your mother?' Gavin looks at each of us, expectantly.

We're not the praying kind. So, we simultaneously gather damp handfuls of soil. Tony says nothing, as he drops the soil around the urn. I step over to sprinkle my soil, too. With a thought for Mum – *I hope you've found what you've been longing for* – I watch the soil bounce off the canister lid's typed label.

'Hang on a mo, Gavin. Why are we burying ashes belonging to someone I don't know?'

I want to throttle Gavin's scrawny neck. He deserves to be stuffed into Mum's half-metre-square burial plot. *I think I've converted that correctly.* I've never been so riled. Before I leave Sutton Road Cemetery, I vow I'll punch Janice and Gwen in their offices.

I'm astounded by the words on the canister. Mum would have been tickled to read:

WITHIN ARE THE LAST REMAINS OF
MRS GLADYS DODDS
1919-2006
MAY SHE REST IN PEACE

PASSAGE

    He was never there to push a pram
        or chair for his passenger daughters.
Conscription robbed him of the wonder
        in their eager faces
        watching the world from the Silver Cross.
When civvies replaced dull uniform,
        his girls had grown strong legs for scooting,
        cycling; sporting grazes,
        Dettol-dabbed, plastered, and kissed better.
He fussed and clowned about to cheer them;
        never dreamt their roles might be reversed.

    His women greeted his last flight home
        from Iberian autumn to damp,
        cheerless November; Christmas, New Year,
        if he should last that long.
They coveted his wheelchair transport:
        made him squeal with fright, delight; raced him
        carefully through the gleaming concourse,
        towards encroaching night.
His tears mingled with smiles of relief
        that his journey was ended, complete.
        More, that he would be fondly cherished.

BRYN MIST
(For Gower artist, Eleanor Williams)

Mist masks the Bryn,
his ancient tracks,
his hollows, knolls;
King Arthur's Stone his mystery.

Mist cloaks the Bryn;
his unkempt scrub
a sodden pelt
protecting his Old Red Sandstone

Mist damps the Bryn.
No song disturbs
cool, pregnant air,
as skylarks feed or pipits preen.

Mist clags the Bryn.
His scents, his smells,
disperse among
ling, moss, bracken, cotton grass bolls.

Mist wreathes the Bryn.
Within the cloud –
his shroud – ewes graze;
haunting forms, fleece palest Payne's grey.

Arthur's Stone

Elegy for Margaret Faithfull – spring blossoms

Mist dissipates.
And Cefn Bryn
reveals his bulk:
his broad backbone –
from where we spy
a muted plaid
of paths, pools, streams –
sprawls in sunlight.
Bright larks ascend, trilling their joy.

WARM NOVEMBER 2011

Gorse in bloom; November.
Nature balmy, barmy.

I remember autumn
days on Gower's coastline:
crashing southerly surf,
foam tumbled by boisterous
gusts; flotsam festering,
waiting for high tide to
sluice its ragged strandline
off sand, shingle, pebbles.

I remember autumn's
icing on raised beach sward:
putrid bracken clothing
Ryer's and Rhossili
Downs, russet horizon
meeting cerulean;
brambles overwhelmed by
winter's grip, decaying
late berries ignored by
stonechats flown south for warmth.

I remember autumn
calm on Rhossili beach
after buffeting gales,
when mini-megalith

pebbles, teed in damp sand,
resembled rugby balls
awaiting a belting
from Stephen Jones's boot
to blast them between posts.

I remember autumn
nights driving up the dim
Common: weaving through wool
turned in on Cefn Bryn's
cosy tarmac, aware
of lights, ruminating;
chasing searchlight full-moon
beams stretching from our Bay
across to Devon's shores;
landing for last orders
at King Arthur Hotel.

I remember autumn,
when Oxwich Point revealed
its naked splendour; its
crags home to tardy house
martins wheeling above
when they need be intent
on winter migration;
fungi replacing spring's
squill-and-primrose patches.

I'll remember this warm
November: hebe spears

windsocks in westerlies;
red campion carmine
on sheltered embankments;
sloes oozing on blackthorn;
bluetits recceing nests
deserted last April
by audacious fledglings;
gorse, golden, in full bloom.

SUNSET, SLEEPLESS

Sun sets in worn grooves
of pin-table horizon.
One tilt west: sundown.

Pockmarked moon face shines
through constellation clusters;
lights up sleepless night.

VICTIM

She has no choice.
She's fed through tubes.
She has no voice.
Her tongue protrudes.
One eye is slack:
can't see the drip.
She's on her back;
can't feel to grip.

She has no tone.
She feels bereft.
She cannot moan.
There's no strength left;
she should have died.
She craves a smoke.
She's eighty-five:
victim of stroke.

MAKING ROOM
(Inspired by an AOL news item)

If you'd scribbled an explanation – a farewell declaration of sorts – things might have turned out different. You never thought of that, did you?

We discussed its likely aftermath: in the gloaming after last cuppa and lights out; ears half-cocked to the daily dawn chorus; skimming skin from our mid-morning cocoa. It was easy to chinwag while day staff busied themselves with bedpans, changed water jugs, or helped someone hobble back to the relative security of bed. I listed potential problems which might affect us both (in clearer script than Maud's, in spite of my Parkinson's) in two columns headed 'M' and 'H'; to confuse any potential readers. The 'M' might have stood for Maud, the 'H' for Harriet. But I wasn't thinking so much of our names; not like for scoring Scrabble or Rummikub. I meant 'M' stood for mine and 'H' stood for hers: problems that is. Not that Maud would experience personal difficulties afterwards, per se. (And that's not a sick joke. It's a fact.)

We both understood, and regretted, Maud's family would be ever so slightly inconvenienced. But, throughout, I reasoned that if it was what Maud *really* wanted, then we'd both be so much better off. The staff here would overcome any publicity, in time. It goes with the job. Circumstances vary. They'd sort it, eventually. (They'd organise a flurry of activities to confuse memories. For instance, we were long overdue community singing with talented Mr Nugent on his Yamaha.)

When there's no alternative, shared accommodation's acceptable. It helps if you're both on an identical intellectual level, though the intimate aspects can be a nuisance (especially when you're left starkers in a hoist, because an orderly's been taken short then has to answer a phone call at the nurses' station). I've never been one for television soaps, which staff linger over using excuses that our room needs tidying. Soaps are time-wasters. I'd hate to have to endure watching Coronation Street. I tired of the series in 1975. Listening's not a problem. No-one's checked my batteries for ages. I manage to answer when spoken to; I'm proud of my lip-reading skills.

The news media went doolally. They reported 'jealousy, conditions, premeditation'. They were unhealthily preoccupied with our ages. It was of little consequence that we were in our dotage; made no difference. Just because we lived in a retirement home, didn't mean we couldn't still reason for ourselves. Didn't mean our nervous systems were shot at. Certainly disproved theories that we were all senile and past it!

And, would you believe, not one of the papers sent a reporter to speak to *me*! (I suppose some editorial was accurate. Her snoring *was* a contributory factor; not just in the night, but in the lounge, in the conservatory, in the fourteen-seater when we livelier ones were bussed to the local garden centre. If I saw her wheelchair parked – couldn't miss it with a gaudy florist's bow attached – I sometimes asked to be moved, just in case the snoring started . . . part of the pretence.)

Last month, Maud had telegrams from the Queen and what's-its-name, the Health Secretary. Very proud she was. A bit choked, too, for reasons she didn't let on about until after her birthday bash.

She'd decided it was high time; that she couldn't stomach Friday's habitual fish and chip lunch forever more. So, like a wand-less fairy godmother granting every wish, I agreed with everything she suggested. Of course, that was all before my batteries failed.

We talked about which method might suit Maud best. I favoured sitting across her mouth, on one of her latex lumbar pillows. (There's not much flesh on my bottom, but I'm around twelve stones, and my hips are wider than most; always the pear-shape, never the hour glass.) All Maud would have to do was lie flat on the floor. I could pretend I'd fallen on her.

We fall a lot. It's easy to drop a boiled sweet – usually, just after you've unwrapped it. It rolls onto the carpet and collects Lord knows what, and when you try to recover it, you inevitably tip forwards and sprawl on the floor. Doesn't matter which chair you've been parked in for the day. The call-button never falls with you, so you lie, as though you're researching into the manufacture of carpet tiles, shouting yourself hoarse, until an orderly finds you and fusses. Inevitably, as though they're suffering the same predicament, they ask 'What are we doing down here, then?' My fleece jacket always comes up looking a mess – goes to show they don't vacuum as much as they should – and that's not accounting for bruises and swellings. Turns out I'm one of the toughies; not broken any bones in all fifteen years I've been in here.

But Maud decided the cord from her towelling gown would be most comfortable, for us both. Lord knows what Maud's daughter was thinking when she bought her old mum Egyptian towelling for that big birthday; probably a result of her being an old mum, too. (I've met all Maud's grandchildren, by the way. They're friendly and caring – all grown up. Like I imagine mine might have been if we'd kept at it; been lucky enough to pull the short straw.) That gown weighs a ton. I tried it on afterwards; much too much weight for any old dear. Felt like I was sporting a shag pile rug. (Candlewick's my favourite. I like to brush its nap in different directions; pick up the light, pretend it's velvet.)

Maud had an extra-large sandwich bag tucked away in her bedside cabinet. The day before the bash, someone had brought in egg and cress sandwiches for high tea. She'd enjoyed the eggs, washed out the plastic bag and given it to me to finish the job; a neat touch I'd never have thought of. That's when I knew she was finally committed, though some might say it was high time both of us ought to have *been* committed!

We agreed it would be bath day, Thursday; creaking hoist, bubbles and talcum, Drapoline, then clean smalls in time for lunch. Child and woman, I've lived life by the maxim you should have clean drawers on daily so that, if you're in an accident, you won't be embarrassed if you have to go to hospital. (Course, if you're wearing a red hat, it'd make no difference: you'd have no drawers on anyway!) So, Maud couldn't have timed it better; sporting silk Damarts stuffed with Tenas, smelling like a pot of hyacinths. I thought, *no-one'd ever guess you've passed the hundred post; kept your own hair and a few teeth, too . . .*

Lunch, on *the* day, was a stodgy pudding – I found just two and a half pieces of lamb buried in my suet – with loads of onions (I'm partial to them), and two scoops of mash a-piece. We agreed it was a miserable final meal for her. But Maud thought she'd have attracted attention if she'd chosen something off the posher menu; it would've been out of character. She was rarely one for rocking the boat. She enjoyed the spotted dick though; drowning in custard it was.

Maud planned to doze off with her gown's towelling cord laid around her shoulders like a priest's stole; ordered, embroidered primroses on each end. Reckoned we'd not be interrupted until around four, when a groaning tea trolley, on its rounds, might warn me. (*She'd forgotten my batteries had failed by then.*)

Maud insisted that, as soon as I reckoned she was unconscious, I was to tie the cord round her neck as tight as I could; her snoring and snorting would tell me when. She hoped she wouldn't have the wind to cry out or fight me off. She hoped I'd have strength enough to maintain the hold on the cord ends, especially if I stood behind her Parker Knoll and pretended I was in a tug-o-war contest. (*I'm ninety-eight. I've not so much as wrung out a bath towel in the past fifteen years!*) Maud said I was to slip the sandwich bag over her head the moment she went all limp, just to make sure. She thought I might like to re-tie the cord over the handles of the bag, just to be certain. So, that's what I did. It worked like a dream; just as she'd imagined. I thought, *shame you can't see the results of all your meticulous planning, Maud.*

She looked awful. Until *my* dying day, I'll never forget that bit. The result? They've arrested me. I've been charged with murder! Murder. *Me*? It was no such thing. I was just helping her; being considerate, kind, compassionate. Maud had had quite enough; had been thinking about all this before her big birthday, but was keen to hang on, just a little while, to read what the Queen had to say to her. *Just a pity she couldn't have left a few words to that effect . . .*

So Maud's timing was ideal, but it caused a stink, in more ways than the obvious one: police crawling over the Home, like horseflies on a fresh cowpat; residents rattled, jittery; rumours rumbling there was a serial reaper prowling the corridors. Worse, that one of our part-time orderlies had suddenly lost it, after bathing the bones and sagging bottoms of a backlog of six old biddies in succession.

Silly old dears! *You're all really fortunate to be in there, 'specially when there's no real alternative and you've no family.* Could be tons worse; maybe *no* lamb in the suet someday . . .

The residents won't notice I've gone. Our room was up the corridor end on Level 2: chairs rarely trundled along to visit, and it was just too far for folks on frames. That's why all our planning was so easy. None of our walls had ears to listen in.

Doubtless they're daily discussing Maud's absence – remembering those lovely flowers rescued from the crem as she went to a better place – chewing Werther's, watching 'Flog It', farting when they reckon no-one'll hear them.

I reckon I'm onto a good thing. And I'm grateful to Maud, for making it all possible. It's not as homely as Room 22 – *two little old ducks* – no soft furnishings or en-suite. There's a lavatory in one corner, so they're installing grab bars for me; grab bars behind bars! That's a joke.

I cope with the early morning calls; used to it after all these years. And I quite like being locked in at night; feels really secure.

The very best thing is – and much more to the point – because of my 'advanced years', I've a room all to myself now.

No more sharing, ever again.

ELEGY
(For Margaret Faithfull, 1913-1998)

Since last
spring blossoms –
in spirited gusts of March breeze –
petalled gravel path and plantation,
(much as snowflakes blanket branch and barren furrow)
you have been patient.

Since last
woodland blooms –
with fragrant mists of bellflower blue –
mottled paths for solitude seekers,
(much as golden-October leaves burnish forest hollows)
you have had to dream.

Since last
harvest fruits –
with showered sunshaft and dewdrop –
waxed full-ripe on laden branches,
(much as ice-beaded webs weigh down skeletal grasses)
you have fought on.

Now,
nature's myriad treasures
bedeck the very essence of you.
For eternity,
gracious lady in repose,
you are at one with your beloved seasons.

CAPTURE

*(A reflection on the congregational response listed in
The Order for Morning Prayer from the
1637 Book of Common Prayer for Scotland . . .
'As it was in the beginning, is now,
and ever shall be: world without end')*

To
glimpse one
breeze-blown snowflake
is to comprehend infinity.
Dismiss sand grains, devoid
of unique design
or breathtaking
symmetry

To those who told me anecdotes for embellishment
to Doreen, who drew pictures, gave shape to my words
to Tony, neglected through two years of OU study
to Jessica, for her stunning limpet studies
to Pamela, Jenny, and supportive writer & reader peers
and to Dr. Wayne E. Thomas

– my gratitude